23 masterfully follows one person's stream of conscious-ness following a traumatic brain injury. Each step of post-TBI growth is visited and tracked, outlining a lucid path that flows easily and naturally. Richly sown with quotations and reflections, it stimulates readers to exam-ine their own experiences. *23* is an excellent faith-based guide for anyone facing adversity of any kind.

—Mike Strand, Author,
Meditations on Brain Injury

23 is an inspirational memoir written from the heart. Articulately drawing on his own experiences, as well as on the words of others who have grown through facing adversity, Dennen offers tremendous courage and hope.

—Michelle D. Sherman, Ph.D., Psychologist,
Finding my Way: A Teen's Guide to Living with a Parent Who Has Experienced Trauma

Nicholas Dennen lives by the motto, "As we learn, teach, and as we teach, learn." A student and a teacher, Nicholas, reflecting on his own experiences, including his near-death experience, helps us to recognize the importance of making the right choices before it is too late. His story, words, and insights are powerful. He makes us think about the eulogy we would want someone to say about us, and he encourages us to live that way today. It is time to choose our paths and live.

—Kian K. Dwyer, Author, *Living Your Chosen Eulogy: live today how you want to be remembered*

23

TIME TO CHOOSE

Bonnie &
Gale, Anything is possible if you
Believe!

TIME TO CHOOSE

God Bless,

Nichole P. Dennen

DENNEN

Beaver's Pond Press, Inc.
Edina, Minnesota

Coming Back, Comfort from the Past, Terror at 3 A.M., Song of Courage, More than Second Best, Surrendering to the Process, Keeping Your Perspective, The Hero's Response, Believing without Understanding, and *Impossible Possibilities* are reprinted with permission from *Suffering Loss, Seeking Healing,* by Evan Drake Howard. © 1996; all rights reserved. Published by Twenty-Third Publications, New London, CT 06320.

"The Paradoxical Commandments" are reprinted with the permission of the author. © Copyright Kent M. Keith 1968, renewed 2001.

"Have Positive Thoughts, and Always Hang In There" by Douglas Pagels from *The Language of Positive Thinking.* Copyright © 1999 by Blue Mountain Arts. Reprinted by permission of Blue Mountain Arts, Inc. All Rights Reserved.

"Help Yourself Reminders," from HELP YOURSELF by Dave Pelzer, copyright © 2000 by Dave Pelzer. Used by permission of Dutton, a division of Penguin Group (USA) Inc.

Taken from **Purpose Driven° Life** by Rick Warren. Copyright © 2002 by Rick Warren. Used by permission of Zondervan.

ISBN 13: 978-1-59298-145-8
ISBN 10: 1-59298-145-3

Library of Congress Catalog Number: 2006908645

Printed in the United States of America

First Printing: October 2006

10 09 08 07 06   5 4 3 2 1

Beaver's Pond Press, Inc.

7104 Ohms Lane, Suite 216
Edina, MN 55439
(952) 829-8818
www.beaverspondpress.com

To order, visit *www.BookHouseFulfillment.com*
or call 1-800-901-3480. Reseller discounts available.

Dedication:

23 is dedicated to my family, my friends, and those who endured my pains and struggles with me. It is for my parents, Jack and Patty Dennen, and my sister, Natalie, as well as for my grandparents, Dorothy and Lenny Olson, Jack and Kate Dennen, and Jack and Flo Welsch; you have given me love. It is for my friend Sean; you have been a brother to me and have always supported my life. You will always be part of my family. It is for my friend Mike (Langriddle); you have given me the confidence to be more than I thought I could be and to strive for those things I didn't think were possible. **It is for all of** my aunts and uncles; my cousins; my nurses; my therapists; my doctors; my fellow patients and their families; my co-workers; my teachers; my advisors; and everyone I've met along the way.

I am forever indebted to all of you.

Contents

CONTENTS

Foreword

I remember the first time I saw him. Sitting in a wheelchair in a hallway, his gaunt man-child body leaning slightly forward, oblivious to the hubbub around him, eyes open but distant, gaze cast downward at nothing, he remained motionless. A woman stood at the back of his chair, talking to his therapist. Her calm warmth spread toward her son as if to soothe him.

The next time I saw him, he was upright, gingerly and slowly walking along a hallway wall with the assistance of a physical therapist, looking even taller and thinner than I remembered, but with a glimmer of concentration piercing the clouds in his eyes. His mind was starting to work, telling each foot to move forward carefully, concentrating to maintain his fragile balance. His mother walked slowly behind, matching his steps, a proud smile beaming on her face, her joy cushioning his every move.

I officially met Nick Dennen months later when he became my patient at Abbott Northwestern Hospital's Sister Kenny Institute Brain Injury Clinic. Ten months had passed since he had escaped death. During that time he had transferred to our hospital, gone from in-patient to day hospital rehabilitation and finally made it to a specialty out-patient clinic through the sheer force of his indomitable spirit and the unflagging support of his dedicated family and friends. He was motivated to improve every aspect of his communication, including his pronunciation, conversational skills, and general use of his voice, as well as his reading and writing. His mother, Patty, became his work partner at home, continuing to be a source of encouragement as well as constructive feedback. Our sessions together at the hospital revealed steady progress in every aspect of his work. The severity of the brain injury still impeded his awareness of some of his limitations and there was no magic potion to speed that up, but he was perfectly clear about his determination to recover as much as he could, including his physical strength and stamina. His eyes shone with dedication and pride when he described his daily progress at the gym near his home, where he worked out like a house afire and met goals like every other athlete there.

Nick wanted to be discharged from our out-patient program five months after we started. Who could blame him? He needed to be back out in society, testing himself in yet unimagined ways, perhaps first by working, then attending school, seeing his friends, and ultimately making a life. He left to begin the next phase of his recovery, and with it the continued integration of his mind with his body and with his spirit. He stopped by to see me every few months, looking brighter and stronger every time, talking more easily and using more sophisticated vocabulary. He began writing e-mails to me, telling me about his life, about college, asking questions about the speech and language aspects of his brain injury, and letting me glimpse his spiritual journey. He sent me inspirational messages that he had found helpful, and eventually our e-mail and in-person conversations took on a collegial nature. I usually tell my patients that, even though I am their doctor and they are my patients, they are also my teachers and I am their student. I learn from everyone I see, and not just in terms of acquiring professional knowledge. However, never before had I the privilege of working with anyone as injured as Nick, who through his rigorous discipline and compassionate desire came to a place where he could write such an inspirational book as 23.

So, welcome to the world of Nicholas P. Dennen, a human just being himself, striving to become the best he can be and giving voice to his journey. You will meet a man who survived a tragedy and lived to tell about it, who unlocked the words trapped within his mind and the feelings within his soul, who laments the circumstances of his injury but takes on the challenge of living aloud. He will take you where he has been and encourage you by showing you the possibilities before you, possibilities you can embrace if you have faith in yourself. He is living proof of Abraham Heschel's eloquent words: "We become what we think of ourselves." He will not speak in platitudes but rather will touch you with his acceptance of his struggle to become whole, and will inspire you with the joyful healing his new life continues to embody.

May peace flow through you like a river.

—Anita L. Kozan, PhD, CCC
Speech and Language Pathologist
Voice Rehabilitation Center
Abbott Northwestern Hospital
Minneapolis, Minnesota

PSALM 23

A Psalm of David

The Lord *is* my shepherd; I shall not want.

He maketh me to lie down in green pastures:
he leadeth me beside the still waters.

He restoreth my soul: he leadeth me in the
paths of righteousness for his name's sake.

Yea, though I walk through the valley of
the shadow of death, I will fear no evil: for
thou *art* with me; thy rod and thy staff they
comfort me.

Thou preparest a table before me in the
presence of mine enemies: thou anointest my
head with oil; my cup runneth over.

Surely goodness and mercy shall follow me
all the days of my life: and I will dwell in
the house of the Lord forever.

(Thomson 1946)

Introduction

When you reflect on your life, what is it that you regret most? Is it all your past failures and what should have been? Is it the times you found yourself fighting for your right to live by your own standards? Or is it the times you should have taken a stand for yourself without giving in to someone else's opinion about how you should live?

Many of us expect that the world will kick us when we are down and that there will be nobody to help us get back up. And sometimes we need to accept this reality. However, after experiencing what was supposed to be the final round, I found a support system united to offer me strength when others thought that my return to life would be impossible. *23: Time to Choose* tells of the strength found in the hearts of many adversity-bearers who offer themselves as bridges into the light.

Choosing a path that is often abandoned because it is hard to walk on is always fulfilling. It's a heroic path, and choosing it gives a person the confidence to accomplish difficulties with ease. And what one may deem impossible, another may view as a hidden opportunity: a gift. But to succeed in moments of despair, you have to eliminate all negative self-talk. You can reach the end of the difficult path only when you have the right attitude. Trust in your heart, and you will triumph.

23: Time to Choose symbolizes life over death, possibility over impossibility, moving forward over slipping backward, having heart versus giving up. It represents seeing yourself, against all odds, dancing that victory dance after many had ruled you out from the beginning. It represents you against you, and seeing that someone else's "opinion" doesn't matter.

23: Time to Choose tells my story of defying the odds, of surviving and flourishing with a traumatic brain injury. My rehabilitation wasn't supposed to help me truly reclaim my life, but it did. It wasn't supposed to further my ability, but it did. And it wasn't supposed to give me the opportunity of a lifetime, and it did. What it has given me is nothing less than the extraordinary, the divine. *23: Time to Choose* offers you inspiration as you search for the genuine "you," the part of yourself that can see the good and that never quits, even when situations get tough.

This book will offer you an outlook that I realized only after much doubt and unrelenting uncertainty. You will see the miracle in life, as I realized that I could only become my best self after having experienced harsh realities. You will recognize that you, too, are capable of deliverance from personal oppression and that you can move into a fulfilling future.

The title, *23: Time to Choose*, manifests in itself the ability to persevere through self-doubt, the doubt of others, and the excruciating pain of dealing with the serious losses that one may experience because of the traumatic events life sometimes gives us. In discussing this endeavor in writing and publishing with my father, he has given me many personal anecdotes I use spiritually, to find God's place in all of it. *Time to Choose* became the subtitle after my father told me details of his first sight of my broken body in the ICU at St. Luke's Hospital in Duluth, Minnesota.

Instead of breaking into a million pieces, his heart felt calmness after he requested God's grace to save his son. He later told me that you can't have courage without fear, and, by turning to God, his fear of losing his son disappeared. My courage spoke for itself as I soon made improvements and was stable enough to transfer to Minneapolis. I was home.

Facing rehabilitation, I realized that what was placed in front of me was a *time to choose*, to choose between persevering over my weaknesses or surrendering to my extreme injuries. It was obvious that the choice I faced would be defining. Nothing in life worth achieving ever comes without a price, and the price I paid wasn't a penalty, but a trade to get something better.

It is my hope that reading *23* will offer you inspiration during traumatic times. By reading what others have offered me, you will feel a sense of achievement and a power knowing that others have persevered through similar trials. The Lord is our shepherd, and He will carry us through the most difficult times in our lives. And as we walk through the valley of the shadow of death, our fear will not be exposed, but our perseverance and courage will. Always remember that your attitude will be a silent strength in your life, and moving forward despite the obstacles you face will be your legacy. We all will have to face a *time to choose* our futures, so rid yourself of all self-defeating anxieties. Fear not, and choose to live.

ONE

In the Beginning

Coming Back

O God of great reversals, who brings day out of night,
Spring out of winter, life out of death,
I seek a turning point as I strive to come back from my loss.
I have been foundering for too long.
I am like a ship in a storm
Trying to find my way back to port.
>   *The howling wind, the driving rain,*
>   *the crashing waves of sadness—*
>   *they buffet my soul and threaten to sink me.*
>   *Is it possible, O God, to be in the storm*
>   *without letting the storm be in me?*
I ask not for protection but for perseverance.
Making it to the safe harbor of recovery
means following you when I can't see where you're leading.

May I keep following in spite of my doubts,
that I may learn that doubt is not the opposite of faith,
but an element within faith.
Certainty is the opposite of faith.
Lead me on, precious Lord, when uncertainty
obscures the way ahead.
Help me to interpret setbacks not as defeats
but as nurtures of resiliency.
Aided by this interpretation,
I am continuing to come back from my loss.
Go before me, O God, that the storm may be stilled
and I may find rest in your embrace. Amen.

—Evan Howard

On a day that changed my life forever, my heart began learning about its life's purpose. This was the beginning of the rest of my life, and reading my story may be the beginning of the rest of yours. My name is Nicholas Paul Dennen. I was twenty when I began this arduous journey on a steep cliff in Duluth, Minnesota. I was in my junior year of college, playing football at the University of Minnesota-Duluth, and learning life's lessons. This is my take on, and my attitude towards, the stages people face when confronting adversity: denial, anger, bargaining, depression, and acceptance. I never imagined something so dramatic would happen to me, that I'd question why it happened, that I'd promise that I'd be OK if my family and I won in court, that I'd not give a damn where life took me, and finally that I'd end up with the attitude that I could tackle anything. I never imagined I'd be able to live with a traumatic brain injury (TBI) and the mind-body experience I now have.

Storyline: It is 1:30 a.m., September 27, 1998. This is how I "imagine" the night happening. I am at the scheduled home game football party. There are multiple kegs. I am getting drunk since I haven't yet learned how to drink responsibly and control my alcohol. The cops are here. I panic. Dammit; my roommates must've escaped. A police officer tells me to get in line. But I sneak off and head upstairs; I can't get another underage drinking ticket. I find a bed; I crawl underneath. A flashlight creeps over the shadows, finds my feet underneath the bed. I am told to get out; I go downstairs. I get in line, get my underage consumption ticket; or maybe I don't. I have no memory, and know just only what I've been told. I'm sure I am upset. I begin walking home.

This is when I meet the man who would change my life forever, who would unknowingly alter my life, and ultimately transform my future; who would start a chain reaction of events resulting in displays on my part of indomitable strength, steadfast perseverance, and unlimited heart. I eventually learned from a police report that I was chased for no other reason than the fact that I appeared suspicious to the officer. I was chased by the officer and his K9. It appears by the officer's own report that the K9 was "off leash," and had to be "called back" by the handler.

It appears that by trying to avoid contact with the officer and his dog (I don't really know if I had contact with the dog or not) I fell thirty-five feet down a cliff into a creek. The officer radioed for water rescue, and three other men saved me. Note: the officer who played a deciding role in my fate didn't attempt to save me. I suppose he froze in shock given the circumstances. A thirty-five-foot fall plus a near drowning must have been beyond his comprehension. For my part, the fall, and the near drowning left residual scars, the kind that only walking a road-less-traveled can produce.

The rescue was complicated. Since I was thirty-five feet down, a fire truck had to be requisitioned to get me from the creek to the ambulance. I imagine that, as the medics continued CPR, my meeting with God was under way and our strategy was surely unfolding. Though my life nearly left me, the certainty behind my faith spoke for itself as my shallow breathing slowly returned.

My mom wrote down her recollections of learning of the accident and feelings about the event that followed.

Sunday, September 27, 1998.

4:44 a.m. Looked at digital clock; phone rang. A man introduced himself as the chaplain at St. Luke's Hospital in Duluth. He asked if I was Patricia Dennen—yes, was I Nick's mother—yes. He told me Nick was involved in an accident and that he wanted me to talk to the ICU nurse. I asked what happened and asked him to wait until Jack could pick up the phone. He told me Nick had abandoned his vehicle and fled the police and fell thirty-five to forty feet into Chester Creek. The nurse gave us a brief description of his injuries and we left immediately. Natalie also answered the phone at the same time.

8:00 a.m. We arrived in Duluth and were told Nick was in surgery with the neurosurgeon to put a monitor in his brain.

12:00 p.m. Noon. Dr. K. came to talk to us before we could see Nick. He told us about the head injuries from the fall and also the near drowning. He told us about the lung injuries and possible spinal injuries. The x-rays were not back yet. He also told us that he did not know exactly what happened but we may have to deal with charges being filed against Nick.

Nick's roommates came up late in the afternoon and we found out Nick did not have his vehicle out that night. It was at his house. Now I wondered whose vehicle he was in.

About 5:00 p.m. The police chaplain and lieutenant came to talk to us. I remember telling them that Nick's car was at his house and asked whose car was he in. I didn't get an answer. They really didn't give us any info. I went on about them chasing kids and causing this—Jack got me to stop.

I also asked them for the name of the officer who had saved Nick—I was led to believe it was the same man chasing him. They said they would get back to me. They never did.

Thursday, October 8th (Twelve days later)

I met a young Officer outside the hospital. He had stopped and asked Grandpa Jack if he was lost (he was pacing). They talked and the officer told Grandpa Jack that he was one of three officers who had jumped down to save Nick. I came outside at that time. He let me know also that he was not chasing Nick but had responded to the call. He told me he thought Nick had been in the water no more than five minutes. He also told me that when I was ready, I should get a copy of the police report. I sent Grandpa Jack to get it right after the officer left. He also asked if he and the other two officers could come up and visit. They never did.

So for reasons I'll explain, my family and I decided to sue the city. Our lawsuit was the attempt to make things right through the efforts of our fearless attorney, a man I'll call, Ezekiel 25:17. Regardless of what ultimately happened, pursuing the suit helped me come to the hard truths about the world, reality, and struggle, and opened my eyes to the purpose behind my life. By living with integrity, recognizing everything that was possible, and surrendering myself to a life developed through difficulties, I've seen *23* emerge.

After the events of the accident, the lawsuit, and my initial recovery, I had to ask what the rest of my life had in store for me. Realizing the abundance of help-yourself books, I thought if I wanted to write about my experience, what could I offer? Who could I serve? Due to an initial lack of confidence, I pushed everything back to the depths of my consciousness, which resulted in insecurity, hopelessness, and mental chaos. I soon discovered, though, stories of people who, because of their horrific experiences, walked paths similar to the one I was on and discovered something about themselves, namely that they now could see the purpose of their lives.

I made a few self-realizations and decided to go outside my comfort zone. You see, I had been so wrapped up in the problems I had and the things I didn't have that I had become my own worst enemy. I was missing the entire picture; I didn't quite understand myself—yet. Then I began to write.

Writing this memoir has given me the opportunity to tell the world what I have learned, while offering great insights from others that I've come across throughout my journey. These insights have come from inspiring passages, speeches, and indescribably wonderful readings, not to mention the advice of countless others who have shared their experiences with me. Because of them I have learned that the values, desires, and passions I truly cherish were hidden from me prior to my accident and recovery. And through the guidance of others, I became obsessed with developing my post-TBI self. It is my goal to sincerely describe how I came back from the arms of darkness and came to see my accident as fortunate.

Christopher Reeve, known for his film portrayal of Superman, wrote about his life and the trials he faced after becoming a quadriplegic ten years ago: "It seemed to me that the values embodied by Superman on the screen should be the values that prevail in the real world." Through Reeve's example, we see that adversity plus courage equals hope.

Trisha Meili, the "Central Park Jogger" who was brutally raped and left for dead in 1989, wrote that life after her rape was about "waking up and living in harmony with oneself and the rest of the world. About cultivating some appreciation for the fullness of each moment we are alive. About not dwelling in the past or wishing for the future." Her subsequent success as a motivational speaker is part of a legacy in hope.

One of my newfound heroes, Kyle Maynard, endures the misfortune of congenital amputation: he has disfigured arms and legs yet succeeds as a wrestler and lives his life fully. His personal motto, and the title of his published memoir, is *No Excuses*. Maynard has shown me that one can, despite insurmountable adversities, overcome an endangered future and thrive. Maynard says, "My experience has taught me that we have no idea how far we can push ourselves, given the will and desire to win. Every time I've come off the mat victorious, I've proven to myself and everyone who has seen it happen what I know to be true: anything is possible."

These courageous individuals have looked at their dire situations and have seen hope. They've discovered that a feeling for others, a belief in working for the common good of society, is the essence of heroism. Walking a mile in someone else's shoes is probably the best way to gain an appreciation for the meaning behind struggle and to accept a sincere relationship with yourself. These brave souls gave me not only hope but my fearless attitude as well.

Dave Pelzer, who endured severe child abuse from the time he was four until he was twelve, is similarly inspiring. In his book, *Help Yourself,* Pelzer offers readers an inspiring vision of personal empowerment, using anecdotes from his own life's struggles with adversity. Pelzer explains how his personal power helped him develop into the man he is today. By portraying himself as a self-willed individual who overcame seemingly impossible situations, Pelzer uses his own experience as a resource to inspire his readers, sharing in his vision of empowerment and encouraging people to live life on their own terms.

Jacqui Saburido, in the US from Venezuela to study English, was hit by an intoxicated teen driver in September of 1999, an accident that altered her life forever and resulted in her receiving severe burns over 60 percent of her body. Her story and advocacy against drunk driving offers hope to everyone, as does Joey Carlson's journey from Olympic speed skater to paraplegic. On August 3, 2000, Joey was driving home from training when a person driving a semi-trailer truck passed, then jerked his rig into Joey's lane, sending Joey's car into the ditch, breaking his neck, and shattering his dreams of Olympic Gold. The driver of the truck stopped, perused the scene, and then took off again.

Aron Ralston chose to amputate his own arm after his hiking expedition in the Utah Canyonlands was stopped short when an eight-hundred-pound boulder shifted, pinning his right hand and wrist against the canyon wall as he hiked through the pass. Ralston says,

"While I've learned much, I have no regrets about that choice. Indeed, it has affirmed my belief that our purpose as spiritual beings is to follow our bliss, seek our passions, and live our lives as inspirations to each other. Everything else flows from that. When we find inspiration, we need to take action for ourselves and for our communities. Even if it means making a hard choice, or cutting out something and leaving it in your past. Saying farewell is also a bold and powerful beginning."

Greatness is found in such brilliant examples of bravery. And like Ralston, I had to cut off a piece of myself, my self-defeating attitude, and leave it behind.

Learning from others who have persevered is my inspiration for *23*. When I first heard Dave Pelzer speak, he was just another guest on Oprah's television show. But as he continued to tell his story, I became inspired; I was drawn to him. What was happening? I was realizing that adversity doesn't have to control your life. Dave was talking about his new book, *Help Yourself*, and I was hooked. I just needed to apply the same standards and beliefs to mine. I turn back to *Help Yourself*, Dave's fourth book, when I need a little encouragement.

The Bible also offers many passages that I've found are more than just meaningful to my journey; they are symbols of my heart. I see their influence now more clearly as I reflect on the direction my life could have taken. I see that my focus was misplaced both before and right after the accident. The first line in Psalm 23 says, "The Lord is my shepherd." Knowing He will accompany me has helped further my progress, not only spiritually but also emotionally. It was my responsibility to stop wasting my time on earth focusing on the wrong things. Was the accident meant to happen? How strong was I? Where did my focus belong? My responsibility was to answer these questions.

Writing my story was something I felt obligated to do. Keep in mind: I am not a psychologist or a counselor. I am not a doctor, and have not studied how people adjust, cope, or heal in the face of tragedy. I do not have a license and am not certified to help maintain someone else's mental stability. I can't tell you for sure that if you do exactly as I did, you will succeed as I have.

Nevertheless, it will be a start if you discover a reason to stop feeling sorry for yourself. My spirit is about believing, not seeing; believing in the power of uncertainty, knowing that whatever happens, I would undergo a few psychological and spiritual changes that would ultimately build my self-image and surely strengthen my character.

I will admit that I was skeptical at first, and thought that writing about my life wasn't possible. So many experiences changed that perception. I read Stephen King's *On Writing*. King claims, "Writing is not life." I was somewhat concerned after reading that line, but gained reassurance when he added, "But I think that sometimes it can be a way back to life." Exactly; I want my story to not only benefit me, but to help those who stumble on similar paths, or those who want to discover the essence of triumph over adversity.

Stephen King is known for his remarkable ability to write amazing stories. I think his ability to teach the art of writing is equally as valuable. I would never have written as much as I have, or with as much quality, without his guidance. For that, I am grateful. I hope he can know that my writing began by reading some of his. I appreciate his disclosure of the event that almost took his life. In a sense, I feel a close connection with him. I often think that maybe his accident encouraged him to write about writing, which in turn encouraged me to write about my accident. Isn't it amazing how things develop?

This endeavor has opened my eyes and filled my heart with something that's been missing all my adult life, especially since my accident. Writing is an excellent way for me to sort through the conflicting feelings such as the fear, loss, or anger I have struggled with since I became aware that I was not dead. When I saw my friends relocate, start families, or begin their careers, I saw where I wasn't, and feeling sorry for myself became routine. But I was going to therapy, I was relearning skills, and I was meeting people who would eventually introduce me to living a life based on purpose, not my own self-serving desires.

It's true: no one knows what will happen until it occurs, and no one truly knows how one will manage adversity until it arrives. How to cope? How to thrive? How to get your life back? It's really a matter of learning, developing, enduring, planning, and restructuring your life the way you'd like it, and more importantly, the way you deserve it. King suggests writing exactly how you feel, without worrying about the impression others may or may not get. Write the way you feel, and don't jeopardize your integrity for the sake of pleasing or appeasing others.

My complicated story unfolds in twenty-three chapters. Each chapter explores a wide range of thoughts and ideas, some my own, some from other people, and some a combination of both. I have included excerpts from other people's writings that I have collected over the years. Some are from newspaper articles, some are biblical passages, others are stories I found while searching for the life I thought was abruptly taken from me.

It wasn't a coincidence that I wore the number 23 on my UMD Bulldog jersey in 1998. Not only was that the number I wore in football, but 23 was also the number of the unit where I did my rehabilitation, Station 23, of the Sister Kenny Institute in Minneapolis, Minnesota. And as fate would have it, Chester Creek is one of 23 creek ravines running through the city of Duluth. In fact, this number represents more than my past physical and psychological states. Kyle Maynard's quest to become the world's unofficial strongest teen required him bench-pressing 23 repetitions for the record, and his high school wrestling record concluded with twenty-three wins and eight losses (23-8). Coincidence? I don't think so.

The stories from the Bible that represent hope and overcoming adversity just happen to be Psalm 23, Job 23, and Proverbs 23. Twenty-three is about overcoming struggle, accomplishing difficult feats, and doing whatever is necessary despite the difficulties.

When I think about the significance of this number, I am flooded with memories of events in my life that, had they not occurred as they did, would have made me miss crucial realizations. For example, I wouldn't have met so many others and received their insights. Had I not been injured in Duluth and transferred to the University of St. Thomas, I wouldn't have met Bill McD., my professor of Christian Morality. He is the reason I am driven so purposefully in finding God's place in my life. To actually realize that God has bestowed on me such a worthy and great task, and trusted me with such a responsibility, is something I learned from Bill McD.

This man introduced me to moral principles and to living a life based on purpose. The faith necessary for this has to come from within, from the depths of my soul. My being at the helm of my journey signifies my command and my ability to surmount the odds and prove victorious, despite anything holding me back. Consider Theodore Giesel, whose pseudonym is Dr. Seuss. He showed such faith. He maintained his passion to educate younger generations despite a discouraging start when many publishers rejected his writing. He saw a particular purpose for his life.

There is another reason I wrote this book. I not only needed to sort through a bunch of feelings I had about my life, but I also needed to clarify, in my own words, what truly happened, how my life took what looked to be an unfortunate turn, and how I embarked on a seemingly impossible journey.

When my parents received that phone call at 4:44 a.m. from the chaplain at St. Luke's Hospital in Duluth, they were given the heartbreaking news that I was in the Intensive Care Unit and they'd better hurry, because my injuries put me on the verge of death and only a miracle would save me.

My mom told me they thought it must have been a mistake; it had to be some other young man. Nick would never "flee a vehicle" and run from the police, as they had been told. This story had come from a hospital chaplain, a man of God, so it couldn't have been a lie. And at the time, they didn't think he may have been lied to.

It makes perfect sense that the police may have given a false account of the sequence of events; I suppose doing this kind of thing is necessary when your ass is on the line. But how can the people who are supposed to protect you hurt you? I suppose even police can be wolves dressed in sheep's clothing. I guess people get abused by the system every day and nothing is done; why should my situation be any different?

I call the officer whose canine partner I met on the cliff Matthew 7:15. This Bible verse says, "Beware of false prophets, who come to you in sheep's clothing but inwardly are ravenous wolves" (Matt 7:15). I chose this biblical verse for one striking reason. This man was a police officer; he was supposed to serve and protect, but he did neither. Yes, my impression of this individual is biased, simply because of what happened. It's not inappropriate, however, for what happened should never have occurred, and he did not fulfill his duty.

You might imagine that I have ill feelings towards Matthew 7:15. I did, but not any more. He helped build me up by trying to tear me down. The events he participated in tested my strength and my heart. I experienced a near drowning in Chester Creek and suffered a traumatic brain injury that provided me with a rehabilitation I had to accept, but only if I wanted to live.

I cannot write about this experience without discussing the choices I have made and the corresponding authority they have had in my life. I believe that when something traumatic happens, the choices we make are quite influential on the life we then lead. If you've met a challenge and you want to feel sorry for yourself, that is your choice; nobody, and I mean nobody, is responsible for your response, except you.

Take me for instance. My family and friends could only bring me so far. If I wanted to overcome my difficulties, if I were to rehabilitate, I had to choose to do it. Others could motivate me, offer wisdom or advice, but it was up to me to decide whether or not to accept the challenge. Please remember this one piece of advice, if nothing else sinks in. It's up to you!

Before my head injury, my ability to understand wasn't fragile like it was after. My long-term memory persisted through my initial recovery. My short-term memory, however, didn't. As a result, I had to learn to use a daily planner, which has proven to be something of a godsend. Every day, I record ideas into my cellular phone as voice memos for later retrieval. I write notes to myself; I leave voicemails to myself if I don't have access to paper. I can't take chances anymore with my memory.

I've learned to do these things because I couldn't let the past dictate who I would become or the kind of life I would lead. It has taken me a long time to accept what happened to me, and some days I still don't want to. That is, there are still days when I just want to give up because it seems so unfair. What did I do to deserve this?

I know the accident was just an accident. But what good does dwelling on that do me now? It happened. There is nothing I can do now to change that. I can be upset at the world, angry at my parents, disappointed in myself, but really, what good does that accomplish? Absolutely nothing. That's right, nothing. Suffering has strengthened my resilience; this experience was necessary for me to mature.

Despite what happened, my life is, and always will be, about accepting and overcoming adversity, and living a more productive life, regardless of the setbacks, the struggles, and the difficulties I face. This is my way of finding peace in my life; this is my responsibility, to accept my past as a lesson I simply needed to learn and to leave it at that.

So, what was the hardest part about my entire experience? I can honestly say, without a doubt, it was the psychological trauma I faced. The physical injuries and the lost strength didn't even compare to the traumatic brain injury itself. I could heal, regain the weight I lost; I would slowly, but surely get my strength back. But it was much harder to regain peace of mind.

After realizing where I was and what I'd have to do to rehabilitate, I became depressed, and suicidal thoughts became habitual. I know I could just end the frustration.

Just as I did then, I now ask myself if my life is worth living. I mean, I never go hungry, I have a roof over my head, and I am strong. I think my thoughts of death are further tests. I'm being tested about whether or not I am taking advantage of this experience and serving the world, or forsaking what was given to me.

Mac Hammond, Pastor of the Living Word Church in Brooklyn Park, Minnesota, said that we are wrong in implying that God tests us by such evil means. Those who commit suicide suffer from mental distress. I get disgusted with myself when I think about suicide because I know that I could never take my own life, even though I feel better knowing I have that power.

After all, I also know that I am too strong to let this one event determine the outcome of my life in such a negative way. Wouldn't it be sad if an accident such as mine produced the kind of behavior I detest? I am so often happy beyond words. I also have a lot of things in life I have yet to accomplish. This one event cannot lead me down the path of unfaithfulness. My heart, my passion, my love for the world will help me keep my focus on living.

I need to acknowledge the fact that I am still able to live a productive life. So many people in the world have it so much worse off than I do. Yes, our problems may be similar, but mine almost seems trivial in comparison. My accident could have and should have left me either paralyzed or dead. Instead, I am exercising daily, walking, talking, writing, speaking, hearing, doing everything I enjoy doing, working, playing, and resting.

There are many who are unable to live productive lives because of some Godforsaken disability or sickness. So what is my problem? I have had a detour. That's all my accident was, a mere roadblock. I just need to find an alternate route and finish the race. I must never forget that Rome wasn't built in a day, and I must never forget the alignment between God's clock and ours; they are rarely ever the same.

Though I may work with speed to get things done, God works efficiently and makes sure things are done right. I have always been in a rush, acting as if time was running out. I can remember time and time again my mom telling me to slow down and not be in such a hurry. For example, before my accident I would talk fast. I was always thinking faster than I could say the words. I didn't really consciously slow down until my accident. It took a few years to re-path my speech signals in my brain so that I could speak smoothly. And now, speed isn't as crucial anymore.

I am more and more convinced that God was there with me as I fought for my life in Duluth. It was He who gave me the commitment and ability to build back my strength. I also believe this was His way of changing my focus. His purpose for me wasn't to die at St. Luke's, but forever to lead a life serving others. I've begun to see how strong my *heart* is. That is, I've recognized the personal strength I embody. To me, *heart* is the inner drive to be more than one is or what one used to be. It determines what one will become.

According to Dr. Phil McGraw, author and television personality, *heart* is the "you" that can be found at your absolute core. He maintains that it's all your unique gifts, skills, abilities, interests, talents, insights, and wisdom. It's not your job, your function, or your role. My gifts, my talents, my abilities, and my wisdom are far greater than the difficulties I faced. My heart knew and knows things my mind was and is incapable of knowing, such as how to thrive, or where I ought to apply passion. For some of my recovery, my heart and mind were not working side by side. When my mind considered giving up, my heart said otherwise. It will take more than my past experiences to break me though.

After I regained my mental composure, I struggled with forgiving, forgiving the city of Duluth, forgiving my parents, forgiving myself, and forgiving God. I realized that if I didn't forgive, my difficulties would stockpile, which could have lead to bigger problems. Forgiveness cleanses the soul, and brings you back into alignment with your purpose. It brought me back into alignment with mine and produced feelings of gratitude for what I already had and for how great my life truly was.

There is nothing wrong with being angry, but problems crop up when these negative feelings prevent you from hearing your true calling. I had to refocus my energy toward the greater good and away from bitterness and animosity. Once again, seeing the big picture was crucial. So I have a few hidden disabilities. So what if my life was put on hold for a while? I still have a life.

Most of all, I still have my faith, which is stronger than ever. I can't forget that it could have been worse, so I have faith that I am exactly where I need to be. I see people in a much more compassionate way. My faith urges me to reflect on what might have been had this experience turned to horror. And I reflect on everything that could be possible if I stop resenting the fact that this happened and stop making excuses.

In the film *Remember the Titans,* we are reminded that "Reflection is the better part of a champion." I want to be a champion. I need to be a champion. I am in pursuit of greatness. Through commitment, dedication, and heart, I plan to live a life built of glory and success. I realize that I shouldn't keep what I have experienced and learned to myself; I must share it with others.

Sometimes I think that I am not old enough to be passing along wisdom. Perhaps I should replace the word "wisdom" with something more appropriate to my age. How about "insight?" Perhaps "awareness?" These also express my passion to join hands with those who are in pain, with those who have lost faith, or those facing utter extinction. I need to do God's work. I need to stand for something. This is my promise to you, to the world, and more importantly, to myself.

Brain injuries are often misunderstood. I feel that I am in an excellent position to educate people about TBI. Why? Because if you look at me, I don't look like I have any sort of disability. And many people who have suffered a TBI are in a similar situation.

To the normal eye, I look great. I am in excellent health, I am fit, I am strong, and I can do most things without too much of a problem. But that's the "Nick" seen by the outside. You wouldn't know that I have fatigue issues, where experiencing too much too fast saturates my brain and makes it hard for me to concentrate; or that I learn differently, since relying on my memory fails me more often than not; and that I experience subtle weaknesses, like being unable to maneuver through a crowded restaurant where balance is crucial in avoiding obstacles.

From one perspective, my disability, my label, is nothing more than an inconvenience and something of a nuisance. It's only a minor obstacle. In retrospect, this disability has actually strengthened my abilities in more ways than one. I am able to endure the pain of loss, the pain of sorrow, and even physical pain itself, to the extent that the word "tough" doesn't even come close to describing me.

But not everyone with a TBI does as well as I have. I hope to define and destroy some unwanted stereotypes regarding brain injury and make this disease known. I have learned in my short time with a brain injury (and I have to say six years is short, because an injury such as mine lasts a lifetime), that only those who have had a personal relationship with a TBI truly know what this injury is all about. The public knows very little about brain injury and how it influences those who suffer from one. There is so much I have to disclose about this.

Even if we don't share similar likes and dislikes, all people who've had a TBI share problems and share difficulties: not being able to walk, not being able to speak, being unable to write, losing strength in either the right or left side of the body, having trouble swallowing fluids without choking, and losing weight, something which was very hard for me to deal with since I was an athlete. Just after my accident I lost forty-three pounds; I looked sick. I could have dealt with losing five or ten pounds, but forty-three was extreme.

We share similar hospital experiences; similar prescriptions; tracheotomy scars; head injuries; breathing tubes; physical, occupational, and speech therapy; expressive dysphasia; wheelchairs; transfer belts; psychologists; feeding tubes; thickened liquids; diapers (yes... I wore diapers); hair loss; scars; doctors; social workers; not to mention fear, anxiety, frustration, self-pity, and loss. What about feelings of worthlessness? The list is endless.

At least I had the opportunity to come back. My timely rehabilitation was a learning experience, and a particularly needed one. I was able to get back on track. Everybody has setbacks, and everyone fails sometimes. It was getting back up that truly mattered. I needed to learn about humility, integrity, and about the true strength of my heart. I missed a lot of the things my friends were doing when I was in the hospital and in rehab. But then I consider everything I experienced that they missed. It truly was an extraordinary experience.

"Impossible is just a big word used by small men who find it easier to live in a world that they were given than to explore the power that they have to change it.

"Impossible is not a fact; it is an opinion. Impossible is nothing."

(Adidas Ad)

TWO

Worst Case Scenario

Traumatic brain injury...my TBI. It involves so many problems and outcomes. And it has so many survivors, better yet, thrivers. I had very little exposure to TBI until I received my own. I now know that brain injury is the leading cause of death and disability in children and young adults under the age of thirty-four. Prior to my bad fall and near drowning, I had been familiar with injuries such as concussions and strokes, but nothing this extreme.

Claudia L. Osborn describes head injury in her book *Over My Head: A Doctor's Own Story of Head Injury from the Inside Looking Out.* Upon writing this, she was a forty-two-year-old doctor and clinical professor of medicine suffering a traumatic brain injury that left her struggling to find her place in the world. She proclaims,

"A TBI is damage to the brain that is not degenerative or congenital in origin but was caused by external force. TBIs commonly occur in vehicle accidents, falls, assaults, and sports injuries. When there is rapid acceleration and deceleration of a head, as can occur with a sudden impact to it during an auto accident, the brain is bounced back and forth against the inside of the skull causing bruising and later swelling. Nerve fibers can be stretched and torn diffusely throughout the brain causing physical, cognitive, and behavioral impairments."

The news tells of many recovery stories and facts regarding TBI. Approximately one in four adults with a TBI aren't able to return to work one year after the injury; one year after mine I was still in therapy, struggling, fighting, still enduring.

After reading and hearing many of these "success" stories, I have come to be strongly critical of them. The news often makes a recovery such as mine out to be an easy victory. You go to a few therapy sessions, you take a behind-the-wheel class, you figure out the new you, realizing you look perfectly fine and have a killer smile. However, my smile that first year was lopsided due to the paralysis on my right side. The true story behind traumatic brain injury isn't told on television and in the papers. Things aren't always represented realistically in the media.

Yes, I am back, but you didn't witness the many months of therapy, self-reflection, and hours of unavoidable hard work it took to return. My recovery didn't happen overnight, and it didn't happen without the right guidance. As I said, the news makes having a brain injury seem like having a broken arm. Believe me, I've had both, and they are nothing alike. A broken arm heals in a matter of months. A damaged brain, such as the one I had, takes years to heal. That's right, years. Not months. Not even a few months. Years. And there's no saying you'll ever even get remotely close to being the same person.

Claudia Osborn also writes, "Significant injury can occur without a loss of consciousness, but usually, in a TBI, the brain stem is injured and produces a period of coma that may last a prolonged time. Not all outcomes of head injury are obvious, which is why TBI is called the silent injury."

So many individuals experience the aftermath of a TBI; this fact is often overlooked. Having one is more than just having an injury; it is having a specific way of life. Since TBI is relatively unknown, I wanted to do something; I needed to do something, so I am writing my story. Think about it. The estimated cost of TBI is about $48.3 billion per year. And who do you think is paying for all this?

During therapy, I was able to re-live my life, from the time I was a baby, through childhood and adolescence, to finally, slowly, becoming an adult again. Nobody really wants to relive his or her childhood, but I had to. Having to relearn how to use my fine motor skills was an overwhelming struggle. I could picture the task, but couldn't do it. As fun as reliving your youth might seem, I had no desire to have somebody wipe my ass again, comb my hair, or get me dressed for the day; I just didn't.

How do I feel about that now? It is a lesson that maybe I had to learn, and maybe I didn't. I had no choice. Forget about what could have been, forget about the Nick before the accident; this is my life now, my choices, and my story. Early in my rehab I learned about a man named Mike Strand who wrote articles for the Brain Injury Association of Minnesota. When I first heard of Mike's writing, I was still in the denial stage and didn't want to acknowledge the diagnosis I had been given. As I was in my teen years, I wasn't in tune with reality and the value of personal relationships. Mike eventually published a book about brain injury called *Meditations on Brain Injury*.

And after recognizing the truth about what we had in common, I decided to order a copy. Mike offered a perspective that I needed to accept: "Much of it I would not have chosen, much of it I would not give up." Being unaware of the gifts I was given was a burden, as if I didn't think I could be the man I was capable of becoming anymore. The way I initially saw myself was simply an illusion. In truth I had more of me to re-create and more to obtain with my life than I even had before.

If only I knew back then what I know now, things might have been different. Yeah, if only. All the "if only's." Such an easy thing to say, right? If only I had discovered the possibilities that truly existed early on. I guess, with hindsight, we always say this. I am just so extremely fortunate that my head injury wasn't degenerative, and that my brain could return to its normal capacity. Yes, I can do more now.

You could say I was in rough shape the day I arrived at St. Luke's Hospital following the water rescue and near drowning in Chester Creek. I don't remember anything of that day, or the next day, or the next. I don't remember the previous day, or previous week. All of that memory is gone. I was hospitalized in Duluth for a total of nineteen days, from September 27th to October 15, 1998.

I wish I had been conscious to see that family came, friends came, my University of Minnesota-Duluth Bulldogs came, everyone came. The 'Dogs prayed for their fallen teammate as I lay unconscious, fighting for my life; fortunately my support system proved strong. Severe trauma to my body was evident. Even though I was unconscious, I must have realized that my duty was to focus on the task at hand—to get my health back to at least good if not great. After nineteen days in Duluth, I was transferred to Abbott Northwestern Hospital in Minneapolis, where I became a patient at the Sister Kenny Institute, a highly recommended rehabilitation facility.

My first injury was a closed head injury; my skull was not penetrated, but it was damaged as a result of the force of the fall, which caused my brain to rattle inside my skull. This injury required me to relearn every skill I had previously taken for granted. I was also diagnosed with a pneumothorax, which is a complete or partial collapse of one of my lungs. This was the result of the direct trauma my chest wall suffered, becoming structurally unsound.

And finally, I suffered from pulmonary aspirations, or shallow, rapid breathing the morning I was rescued. I was hungry for air. This, in fact, was far more intense than any collision I ever faced on the football field.

Due to my injured lungs, I was manually ventilated at the accident site, and a tube was placed down my throat. And like a vacuum cleaner, a suctioning device was used to remove secretions I was unable to cough up but that guarded my body from infection. When the tube was no longer able to travel down my throat, I had to have a tracheotomy, a tube surgically inserted through the center of my throat. Yeah, there is definitely a scar there, which is fairly noticeable. But actually, when I think about what could have happened—how much worse it could have been—a scar on my throat is nothing.

Everyday I see people in wheelchairs, and others who are experiencing far greater difficulties. This really puts the adversity I face into perspective. I also had chest tubes surgically placed through both sides of my torso in the hospital. I suppose a few scars on my body are just everyday reminders of how bittersweet real life can be.

It is truly amazing the technology and intelligence we have. The medical field is increasingly becoming more and more effective in treating severe injuries. I was so extremely fortunate to have received fantastic care at St. Luke's, from both doctors and nurses alike. But I guess in retrospect, I agree with what a character in the movie *The Notebook* says, "Science goes only so far and then comes God."

The (my) brain has created new pathways and is working again. I can't imagine the way some people endure life confined to a wheelchair or being unable to think for themselves. And those are only the disabilities I know about. The brain is such a fascinating machine. It is the most complicated thing this world will ever know. It can do so much and achieve so much. I am grateful for all that I've regained.

It is gratifying to know that I am now writing my story, which will hopefully encourage countless others to achieve what seems to be the impossible. Just knowing that my kind of recovery isn't impossible offers hope to even those who haven't had such an injury, though I wouldn't have gained such an appreciation for personal stories of those who have undergone traumatic experiences had I not undergone one myself.

In the first chapter, I mentioned Kyle Maynard. This young man, on January 5, 2005, offered me the most sincere, most genuine perspective on overcoming adversity. He was featured in an HBO special called *Real Sports* with Bryant Gumbel. His attitude and his zest for life showed me how someone under the most extreme circumstances can live a prosperous life. Congenital amputation hasn't limited his ability but rather has strengthened it, and he offers himself as a shining light for the future.

Maynard not only displays a lot of heart, he has an extremely strong drive, matched by an unbelievably strong attitude. He doesn't quit, especially on himself. He never gives up. His ability to conquer major obstacles really represents for me the courage behind an unbreakable heart. Maynard claims,

"To live with 'No Excuses' means to take a robust, rugged individualistic attitude toward life's problems; it's about freedom and responsibility; it's about hard work and hard choices; it's about self-reliance that is joined naturally with family, friends, community and faith. No excuses is about America as it used to be and should always be."

After seeing him, feeling sorry for myself seemed pointless, and I recognized that I couldn't blame others anymore but had to take responsibility. It was now or never, and I made a choice to accept my life. This is where I should have always been, but embracing this is hard when one is dealing with extreme loss. It took time to develop this awareness about myself. Once I realized what I had to do, though, my life had new meaning.

Did I feel somewhat to blame for the influence my accident had on the people I care about? Of course. My father has mentioned to me that his ability to endure anymore trauma is gone. Dealing with me and the shape I was in took a huge toll on his life. Comparing himself to a cat, he says he lost eight of his nine lives in Duluth.

But after I became more acutely aware of all the different adversities people endure, I saw that my attitude was unreasonable, that it was unreasonable to continue falling victim to self-blame and self-doubt. It is almost like I had been living a dream. I came to know that what I went through is something people have been dealing with forever. I was given a second chance.

It has taken a long time to recognize that I had been telling myself a ridiculous story, a story where having this TBI was the cause of my being stuck in the past. Realization: TBI was only an excuse, and shouldn't have influenced me negatively. I realized that this experience was never just about me; it was about my personal relationship to everyone in my life.

I hadn't been aware of all the sickness, all the disease, or all the pain in life. I recognized it, but I didn't feel it. I wouldn't have felt this level of gratitude before my accident, the kind I am feeling right now as I write my thoughts, because I was going through life on a straight path: no curves, no bumps, just a flat road. It was these bumps in the road that shaped and molded my individuality and taught me a lot about myself during my two-year rehabilitation.

What I found was a life-changing perspective that will guide me to living my life aligned with God. I want my work, my life itself, to be representative of my passion, something I can use to ignite my entire being, without question. My life will inspire, encourage, and offer passion. This is how I will be defined. Remember, the negativity behind TBI is just the story I was told, but "prevention" is the only known and sure cure. So please, from the bottom of my heart, I ask you to be safe.

"We must all suffer one of two things: the pain of discipline or the pain of regret or disappointment."

(Rohn 2006)

THREE

Unexpected Gifts

Comfort from the Past

God of every time and place,
grief sends memories rippling through my mind
like the windblown water of a mountain lake.
    The good times and the bad times
    are part of my inner world,
    part of the spiritual experience
    that makes me who I am.
My memories can make my heart tender;
they can also bring it encouragement.
May I receive every good memory as a gift of your grace.
    I close my eyes and see faces now gone,
    streets and homes now changed,
    images of myself now transformed from youth to maturity.

Thank you that I have much to treasure from the past.
Although my loss has devastated me,
I won't let it take everything.
> *The special moments I have known*
> *still burn brightly in my spirit. I reclaim them now.*
Thank you for the wonders of my childhood—
the grass beneath my feet, the adventures with friends,
the discoveries made in school.
> *Let me not forget the successes I enjoyed*
> *in growing up, which infused my spirit*
> *with a sense of inner approval.*
Most of all, bring to my mind the relationships
that have sustained me across the years.
May I find new people with whom to share my life now,
that memories of today will comfort me in the future
as I am comforted today by memories of my past. Amen.

—*Evan Howard*

What we say to ourselves is extremely important as we attack any battle head on. I am a huge advocate of positive reinforcement and mentally challenging myself during my everyday struggles. Considering the burden I faced fighting my way through the trauma, the most important thing that helped me deal with it was my inner conversation with myself. I'd ask myself, "Are you going to let this single event, this one moment of despair, ruin your life, or will you persevere and prove all those critics wrong?" People who were skeptical about my ability to recover suggested that because I was weak, I would never return. In the end, they really stood no chance of being correct.

It's actually pretty disheartening when I'd reflect on how I would beat myself up, telling myself how bad my life was, or that I didn't even deserve to live. I get disgusted now when I remember my attitude. I mean, seriously, if I didn't believe in myself, it would have been hard for others to believe in me. Each of us should be the first person in the ring sticking up for ourselves. During the early days of rehab, I was distraught; I was mentally disturbed and had a hard time valuing my life.

I wasn't keeping myself in check against my negative self-talk. Like everything, changing my attitude toward myself became mind over matter. My primary physician, Dr. Smith, told me that overcoming such a trial was really about harnessing the mind and the spirit. It was about being elastic and being able to endure the worst. What we say to ourselves and how we interpret our deepest feelings determine so much of our futures. It's the difference between winning and losing, or in my case, between living and dying. I am almost certain it was. What it really came down to was how badly I truly wanted to continue living.

While I was battling to define my place, I was stuck between hating where I was in life and accepting my situation for what it was worth. I remember lying on a cushiony mat in the rehab part of Sister Kenny, unable to walk; I knew I could either choose to stand myself up or remain on my back there in captivity. Yes, this was a hard decision, especially since I was stubborn. But I began to see the answer when I considered looking at myself in the mirror and having to admit to myself that I was only ignoring the truth. I thought I deserved something special. It was then that I decided that I was going to walk on my own, without a cane, without a walker, and declare to the world, in a single moment, that I would not continue without a fight. At that instance, I took that first step; I took a stand.

After transferring to Sister Kenny in Minneapolis, I faced severe problems. Believe me, as a young, strong, resilient twenty-year-old, I found it a very humbling experience to have to have someone else wipe me after I went to the bathroom. Talk about humility.

My doctors and therapists said it might take me a long time to figure things out or learn something new. I couldn't accept that. I didn't want to accept that. I felt I was the same person I was prior to the fall, but I also only saw my physical weaknesses. What did I have to do to get my life back? Accepting my disabilities was difficult, but it had to happen if I wanted to move forward. I realized that it was OK to take my time. Actually, I had always been in a hurry; slowing things down might not be such a bad thing.

I found myself asking the same questions over and over again when I came face-to-face with the man I saw in the mirror. Who was I? What did I stand for? I needed to consider everything I loved, everything I hated, and everything I regarded as necessary for strengthening myself. What was necessary to making Nick stronger? I needed to evaluate my life from the core, and determine my strengths and my weaknesses. I thought about all my problems, and all too often came to the same, highly irrational conclusion. They were too big.

In reality, my problems only seemed huge, simply because that was what I told myself. I feared losing—to my own lack of belief. I was running the risk of coming close to calling it quits, making excuses, and doubting the power of my cause. I met Kian Dwyer, author of *Living Your Chosen Eulogy*. Kian asks, "If you could give the people of the world a gift, what would it be? What do you want for others?" *23* was it.

I met Kian on Saturday, April 30, at a book signing at a bookstore in Minneapolis. When I walked into the store, I made eye contact with Kian, who was some twenty or so yards away in the middle of the store. We both smiled. As I approached her, she greeted me with a friendly hello and we had an instant connection. After discussing her book, I asked her about the entire book publishing process. I wasn't all that confident that *23* was possible. It was at that moment, when I first met Kian, that I knew without a doubt the power behind giving my story to the world. Others could benefit from what I could give.

I wish all young people would learn a bit of humility before it is too late so they can appreciate everything they have and how great their lives truly are. So many people have a severely negative perspective about what it means to be a human. I have met my share of people like this, and I don't ever want to be anything like them. They treat people poorly while disrespecting humanity. This is not a life; humility teaches otherwise.

What I have learned: life will always be about personal relationships. During my recovery, my cup always seemed half empty. It took seeing the power behind my relationships to focus on the half-full half. I saw that my lack of confidence was a disability in its own, a disability within a disability. This lack of confidence restricted me from doing my best and created nothing but doubt. Could I do this? Was I strong enough? My low self-esteem ultimately ignored every new possibility.

I had always listened too closely to what my head was telling me, while not giving enough attention to my heart. I realized that fear of the unknown was holding me back. I had to realize that I had no right sharing my vision of empowerment with others if I sold myself out, if I didn't practice what I preached.

I am here to show the world that there is no such thing as the impossible, that potential does exist amidst the concentrated chaos. It's just a matter of doing what's necessary to make what seems impossible possible. Of course there will be those who'll say that it can't be done. But this world is full of individuals who wrestle with the critics and those who say some things aren't possible. I want to be that bridge joining both limitations.

I have been lucky enough to have met some pretty remarkable people in my life. Whether from the hospital, high school, college, or even from the gym, each person has contributed something genuine to my life. I have seen good people, and not-so-good people. I have seen the way people treat others, and it is often ugly.

What kind of world have we created? There is murder. Assault. Rape. Road rage. Cruelty. You'd think with all the wars and bloodshed, we'd have at least learned something, like how to ignore our petty differences. It's a scary thought to know that there are people in this world who'll kill other humans for pleasure.

Or consider the person or group who will murder because of a specific religious belief. What is wrong with that picture? This entire 9-11 tragedy is a true horror story: a militant group flying airplanes into an occupied building in New York City for the purpose of teaching the United States a lesson. That's not a purpose, that's something sadistic, something insane.

I remember seeing the planes hit the towers in New York. I was living with my best friend, Sean, in an apartment we shared in St. Paul. I didn't quite grasp the magnitude of what had happened. I mentioned to Sean the difficulties our world was facing but how we needed to focus on our current situations, such as furthering our college educations. That was another problem this brain injury provided; I often had a hard time putting things in proper perspective.

I didn't quite understand the magnitude 9-11 presented right away. Before my injury, if something this tragic happened, I would have recognized it immediately, not hours later, only after it was so highly publicized. At this moment, I felt like an idiot, along with feelings of stupidity and helplessness, all feelings common among the brain-injured population. But

I was not an idiot, or stupid, and I was not helpless. Go figure. It was just another false illusion I'd tell myself.

Then, I only had a sense of how serious the events of 9-11 were. Soon after the attacks, I read an article about a group of men on United Flight 93, who took the power back from the terrorists. Though saving many lives that day, they had to crash the plane, killing all the passengers. They took care of those lunatics who tried to undermine America. Our men took it back; our heroes took a stand.

I now see that these men were fighting for their very own existence and the freedom of the United States. They demonstrated for our entire nation what it truly meant to be an American: protecting life, liberty, and the pursuit of happiness. One of these heroic men actually graduated from the same high school as I did. Tom Burnett Jr., quarterback for the Bloomington Jefferson Jaguars in 1980, joined others and decided to do something about those who were jeopardizing the very thing we fought so hard to maintain: our freedom. Burnett Jr. stood for everything patriotic our country stands for: honor, love, and perseverance.

Burnett was recognized at one of Jefferson's home games, a mere three days after the tragedy. The article in the paper spoke of how Burnett Sr. showed up at the game to honor his son. He must have been overwhelmed with pride in how his son helped overtake the terrorists and crash the plane in southwest Pennsylvania. What a powerful story. Even the first time I read it, I felt a sense of honor, knowing the level of integrity Burnett embodied. It's not a coincidence that Burnett was a Jefferson Jaguar sixteen years before I was.

My own high school football career was disappointing. I did, however, learn invaluable lessons. I learned the value of commitment and sacrifice. I had to accept the fact that I didn't get the chance on the field I thought I deserved, despite the effort I gave in the weight room and practice. So what? It was one of those defining moments that taught me a crucial lesson about life.

Lesson: forget the past. It's history. It wasn't the first time I was knocked down, and it sure as hell wasn't going to be the last. As I reflect on my high school sports achievements, I can only feel a sense of gratitude, despite any disappointments. Perhaps the challenges I faced were actually God exercising one of His lessons.

I often wonder what sort of belief system Burnett had; I wonder how he built up enough courage to make the choice he made. The beliefs and values I've maintained when I was forced to make a decision would forever influence my future. Were they similar to Burnett's? Even though our two situations were worlds apart, they did share similar characteristics.

Burnett was faced with a choice that would change his life forever. I was faced with a similar choice. His would impact the world; mine would impact my life and the people in it. And they were both necessary choices. His choice would receive praise and gratitude from our entire nation. My choice would receive the praise and gratitude of a select few.

If I hadn't been so relentless, I would now have more problems than I could bear and I'd be miserable. I realized that day on the mat at Sister Kenny that making the choice to embrace my battle, while leaving nothing in reserve, was going to benefit me not only in rehab but future endeavors as well.

I had a choice: to either wallow in my own self-pity, bitching about how life wasn't fair, or to change my attitude and accept this challenge without fear. It's still hard for me to go through life wondering about where I'd be had I not made the choice to be fearless.

For a long time, the idea of suicide consumed me; it ate me up inside. I thought about taking the easy way out. Ending my life would surely have eliminated my struggle, my loss, and my pain. But when I finally woke up to my purpose, I went from seeing my cup as half-empty to seeing it half-full. What had changed? It took finding myself again after being lost and feeling forsaken.

My spiritual self dealt with my personal vision of empowerment, discerning between the values and moral standards I had about adversity and faith. I found an improved interest in serving my passion and myself, the person who began walking this road-less-traveled. I looked at my experience facing death, and then dealing with a new individual who wasn't all I wanted him to be. I had to have a purpose that was undoubtedly God-given.

It is when things were darkest that I was able to see this reality more clearly. I witnessed a future, for example, where I was distant from the pressures and problems found in corporate America such as greed and envy. I was made for so much more. I was made to serve His purposes, to serve humanity.

What exactly is His purpose for me? Maybe it involves motivating people, or helping others cope with brain injury, adversity, or tough lessons. When I consider this, I feel a surge of strength. This is God's way of making things right. It's funny how in the midst of so much uncertainty you can find something that's so real, so perfect.

There really are no coincidences. Nothing happens by chance or pure luck. It's almost as if God pulled me from that dirty creek and spoke to me. He looked into my eyes, the windows to my soul. Pictures of me lying in that hospital room showed that my eyes were open, but I was not there; I was somewhere else. The truth of the matter is that even though life could not be found in my eyes, a purpose could.

Would I make it back? That was what everyone was thinking. "Poor Nick" is what people were saying. "Nick didn't deserve this." But wait, everything God does is for a reason, right? Did I deserve this? I needed a wake-up call. I needed something to get me out of the self-induced unconsciousness where I was simply treading water, being complacent about where I was going.

It finally occurred to me that I was still alive to be part of something, something more than working for a living and going through the everyday motions. I realized that to leave an impact, to touch the soul of everyone I encounter, I needed to experience pain and struggle myself, so I could relate. Helping others, reaching those I can teach, benefiting those who can teach me, and meeting those who will leave footprints on my soul make up my purpose.

The purpose I was called to manifest required more of myself than I was even able to comprehend. Remember, your purpose is to serve, not to withhold your gifts from those in need. Never underestimate what you can contribute to each situation, each relationship, or each heart. It's all that will ever matter anyway.

"We are all faced with a series of great opportunities brilliantly disguised as impossible situations."
(Chuck Swindoll as quoted by Dwyer 2005)

FOUR

Hard Times

9/27/98

Purpose. For years, I did not recognize my purpose; my mind was not whole and complete. After experiencing a few defining moments, I gained a stronger understanding about my reason for living. For what and for whom am I alive today? Rick Warren, author of *The Purpose Driven Life*, offers a fitting reflection derived from biblical passages that address the strength of life. Warren emphasizes the importance of knowing that you are not an accident, that nothing happens by chance, and that there are no coincidences.

Warren inspired me to share my story in *23* by saying, "The very experiences that you have resented or regretted most in life—the ones you've wanted to hide and forget—are the experiences God wants to use to help others."

Sometimes a single event changes you, or in my case, you change because of continuous actions done everyday. Sacrifice is imperative; it was necessary. What have I sacrificed? This is a pretty difficult thing for me to identify. I have endured a lengthy rehabilitation process. So what? In my eyes, I have sacrificed a substantial amount of time living at the hospital and going to therapy. I struggled with accepting this, especially after seeing where my friends were. And then, to make matters worse, I felt that I missed the window of opportunity to prepare for and begin a career, or so I had thought.

I know that these "missed opportunities" mean nothing in the entire scheme of things, and that in ten years I might catch up with others my age. Who cares, right? Everyone works on different time frames; I can understand that. I just have a difficult time dealing with the fact that my life was altered because of an aggressive police officer. (Dammit Nick, you are doing it again. You are focusing on the past. You need to let this go. I'm writing, so I guess that's a start.)

I was upset that my parents weren't able to do for me what they had promised, that is, protect me, protect me from that vicious wolf who felt he was justified in letting his canine partner come after me at two-thirty in the morning. He said he feared for his life. I don't think he feared for his life at all, but rather feared having to take responsibility for his impulsive actions. I think he realized that he made a terrible mistake, and figured he'd better come up with a good story to protect his future. What about my future?

Despite still feeling violated, I've been able, through self-talk, to see all the great qualities I now possess and the gifts Matthew 7:15 has actually given me. Taking courses in communication at the University of St. Thomas taught me that this communication with myself can ultimately bring about one of two things: an entirely positive, optimistic attitude, or a negative self-reflection about how pathetic my life was. God was at work again here, disguising crucial life lessons through many of my required college courses.

In the end, I'll see my moments of struggle as what they really are, weak, pathetic attempts to decide my life without my knowledge or my consent. In reality, I am going to give my accident and its negative aftereffects a proper burial in the depths of hell where they belong, along with every negative attitude I've had. I didn't deserve my accident, yet I will take advantage of every opportunity it offers; the challenge has been merely a learning experience, a defining moment in which I chose to shape my future.

My self-worth and self-concept were initially damaged due to the injuries I received and the physical state they left me in. I was hurt, I was demoralized, but I wasn't out. I was not out of the game yet. It was like an automatic time-out, just like the two-minute warning at the end of a football game. Two minutes is a lifetime. So much can happen with so little time left on the game clock. Games are won and games are lost in a matter of seconds. Two minutes, even though it may seem short, can positively or negatively influence the outcome of the battle.

Consider September 27, 1998. When I fell into Chester Creek, my life was at the mercy of God and the one tangible thing that would ultimately determine whether I lived or died was time. Matthew 7:15, even though I compare him to a ravenous wolf, must have been driven to radio for help as he was unable to save me. He panicked, and the men who came to my rescue pulled my head out of the water just in time; if any more time had elapsed, I would have died and departed from this world.

God's purpose did not include me perishing that fateful morning, but does include forever leading a life serving others. The men who saved me symbolize heroism at its best; they were angels in disguise, very much like my nurses at St. Luke's and everyone at Sister Kenny, and very much like everyone I met at St. Thomas. It was as if these three officers were meant to be there, meant to save me, and in a secondary way, save Matthew 7:15.

I honestly don't think he had any idea what could have happened by releasing his dog. I really wish he had apologized for causing my family so much pain. He didn't, which really says something about his character. In all honesty, I don't think I should be the only one accountable for what happened; however, I now know that my shoulders are strong enough to carry anything.

Rick Warren says it best: "It is sad that in God's flock, the greatest wounds usually come from other sheep, not wolves." Even though I compare Matthew 7:15 to a wolf, I realize that he is just a human being like myself. He is a sheep who had the potential to mimic a ravenous wolf. This ability to transform is fairly commonplace in a society that endures the worst from all levels. We live in a ruthless world, don't we?

In my Christian Morality textbook, *Morality: The Catholic View*, Servais Pinckaers writes that, "Man is not primarily a wolf to man, although he can become one." My heart told me to embrace Matthew 7:15. Accepting mistakes is how we grow, and realizing this about this man has taught me so much. His influence was, in the end, positive and useful.

Rick Warren includes a poem by Russell Kelfer titled "Life Purpose Statement" in his book, *The Purpose Driven Life*. The poem pretty much says it all.

You Are Who You Are for a Reason

You are who you are for a reason.
You're part of an intricate plan.
You're a precious and perfect unique design,
Called God's special woman or man.

You look like you do for a reason.
Our God made no mistake.
He knit you together within the womb,
You're just what he wanted to make.

The parents you had were the ones he chose,
And no matter how you may feel,
They were custom-designed with God's plan in mind,
And they bear the Master's seal.

No, that trauma you faced was not easy.
And God wept that it hurt you so;
But it was allowed to shape your heart
So that into his likeness you'd grow.

You are who you are for a reason,
You've been formed by the Master's rod.
You are who you are, beloved,
Because there is a God!

© Russell Kelfer
Discipleship Tape Ministries, Inc.
Used by permission

What I endured was not easy; it was painful. I needed to grow from it. Embracing my experience was necessary, and so I held on tightly. It would strengthen me, and it would allow me to live God's will. I faced the trauma, which required me to endure an elaborate rehabilitation.

Staying true to my purpose was about belief, faith conquering all. Belief in God. Belief in His purposes, and His love. Trust in His vision of who we are and whom we should follow. We are destined to living purposefully. According to Warren, discovering our reason for living by placing our attention on ourselves is wrong. We are required to focus on Him, on His reasoning behind our sacrifices, and on following His paternal guidance.

I now see that, prior to my accident, I was confused. I was doing what I was doing in order to achieve success monetarily, and get recognized. I forgot the part about His purposes, serving others, and relying on passion. But how can it be considered selfish if He's directing our every move? This is where I struggle. Perhaps it is His way of keeping me in check and interested in learning more about His faith and His purpose.

I have been extremely bitter, stubborn, and resentful over the years because I have felt that things should have been handled differently and that my accident should have never happened. I shouldn't have gone through this. I was angry.

A quotation by William Arthur Ward in which I find solace about life's struggles says, "Adversity causes some men to break, others to break records." This is so true. There are endless lists of people who have "broken records" and declared their resilience. Adversity can be a turning point in your life; it can help you realize what matters most and where your heart belongs.

I know I shouldn't have gotten myself into the mess that led to my fall. I think back and question my motives in Duluth. I was trying to gain false friends by living a life distant from my true purpose. The people I came to know were too focused on getting drunk, going to parties, or getting high. These were not the "friends" I was destined to have, simply because their motives weren't parallel to mine.

I wanted the city of Duluth to pay me a big settlement and make all my worries disappear. Where was my focus then? It was on winning a lawsuit that was going to be the cure-all to the event that almost killed me. The accident happened; the past can't be changed. I need to brush myself off, get back up, and move forward. I've been knocked down, but I can dust myself off and stand up on my own two feet.

That first step is hard. But with God by your side, and courage in your heart, victory is within your reach. Sure, you might fail, but at least you tried.

"We move through places every day that would never have been if not for those who came before us."

(Albom 2003)

FIVE

Blind Justice

Terror at 3 A.M.

It's the middle of the night, dear Lord.
Again, I can't sleep.
    Questions besiege my mind,
    exploding my inner equilibrium.
    Fear and dread rampage within me
    like demons on the loose.
My hands shake. A knot grips my stomach.
A cold sweat forms my brow.
    The terror time is here!
To survive this time will require
all of my strength and courage.
I have had challenges before, but never anything like this.
    My world has crumbled.
    I'm buried in the ruins and must find a way out, alone.

Stay with me until the morning, O God.
Be my companion and friend.
Watch and wait with me in grief.
　　Then I will arise from the ruins and discover
　　the new world that awaits me beyond brokenness.
I can't do it without you, Lord.
I need you like I have never needed you before.
　　Here we are, you and me alone in the night.
　　Stay with me until dawn.
As the light comes,
so may your presence enlighten my heart. Amen.

—*Evan Howard*

After a number of weeks and the initial shock of the accident had passed, my family chose to sue the city of Duluth in hope of dissolving the injustice. Perhaps my parents felt that retribution was necessary since I had practically died and was seriously injured. During the process, we had to acknowledge the past and recognize the potential of a realistic future, while simply living in the now. At first, we had been given hope of a victory that was indisputably in the hands of a single judge. I'll tell you now that the hope was false. We can't resent what happened though, because we followed the terms found in our country's legal system and the law is the law, regardless of how ridiculously criminal our opponents side of the story was.

My attorney, Ezekiel 25:17, took the monumental task of going after a city with nothing more than circumstantial evidence. I chose this verse to represent my attorney after seeing the movie *Pulp Fiction*, with Samuel L. Jackson and John Travolta. Jackson's character chose this verse to represent his pledge as a man trying to be the true shepherd, speaking the truth against the tyranny of evil men. As quoted in the film, Ezekiel 25:17 states,

"The path of the righteous man is beset on all sides by the inequities of the selfish and the tyranny of evil men. Blessed is he who, in the name of charity and good will, shepherds the weak through the valley of the darkness. For he is truly his brother's keeper and the finder of lost children. And I will strike down upon thee with great vengeance and furious anger those who attempt to poison and destroy my brothers. And you will know my name is the Lord when I lay my vengeance upon thee."

Ezekiel 25:17 believed in the impossible and in the truth behind what really happened. His courage helped us take a journey that made us aware that it was the world, not just a single individual, that was sometimes unfair and selfish.

During the suit, I felt abandoned and unmistakably thrown to the wolves, despite my lawyer's presence. Escaping defeat proved impossible as the court dates came and passed, and the facts were turned into unbelievable fabrications. Maybe I was out of my mind to think we could actually win. Our only road to travel was to rely on the vague reports of a wolf dressed in sheep's clothing, who in the end really turned out to be merely human.

According to the police report, Matthew 7:15 was on patrol that night. When he drove past me, I was walking in the opposite direction; he claims he noticed something in my hand that I was supposedly trying to conceal. The article in the Duluth *News Tribune* wrote that I then ran and fell into Chester Creek. I think the facts here were misrepresented; the article mentioned nothing of the officer's improper use of his canine or that I did anything illegal, just that I was carrying something.

My guess is that I was carrying my underage drinking ticket that I received, though no one found the ticket. I didn't escape the party without one, as every Duluth police report claimed. All of my "friends" who were at that same party said it was highly unlikely that I got away. I guess I never should have left by myself. I thought I was made of steel, so why did I have to worry?

From our investigation, it was determined that Matthew 7:15's canine was let out of the car, took off running without command, (which was a key argument in the lawsuit), causing me to fall some thirty-five feet to the water, where I nearly drowned.

Matthew 7:15's report of that night is almost fairy tale-like, leaving out any legitimate, concrete statements. Am I surprised? Not really. His ass was on the line, and a lie, just a little fib, would get him off. So of course he looked out for number one, made me out to be a drug addict, and got off. Only God knows what really happened that night. I have no memory. And there were no witnesses. As you might imagine, trying to make a case was incredibly hard and our attempt failed

Ezekiel 25:17 presented an amazing case to the judge, however. He claimed that the actions by Matthew 7:15 were in violation of my right to walk home safely without being pursued for no apparent reason. The judge saw differently. This federal judge's memorandum and order ruled that Matthew 7:15 did not violate my constitutional rights. Then he granted his summary judgment, the ruling, in favor of Duluth. We lost.

I suppose this city, or any city for that matter, must always keeps its best interests in mind. Why should city officials give it a second thought that one of their protectors made a mistake and almost killed a young man? The article in the Duluth paper claimed that I was arrested twice for underage drinking and convicted once. Whoever wrote that article should have done a little more research regarding the facts. These "facts" were, of course, false.

I was never "convicted" of anything; underage consumption of alcohol is a misdemeanor, simply entailing a minimal fine. I admit, I was only twenty years old, I was underage, and I was drinking. But does this admission mean that I deserved to be assaulted, to almost drown, to receive a head injury, rehabilitate myself, and start my life from the beginning?

The article said that toxicology reports revealed the presence of a combination of barbiturates, amphetamines, and an alcohol level of .227 in my blood. OK, when I was face-down in the creek I was at the mercy of God, and my body began to give up. Under those conditions, my body required a jump-start, a boost of drugs to get my system back on the radar that the rescue team administered. So of course my body showed an excess of drugs that were circulating through my system; the paramedics and doctors gave me the medicine I needed to keep my body alive.

Of course I can't remember the events of that day; I might have taken something in the locker room before the game. But if I had taken anything, it would have been a legal substance that you can buy at any local nutrition store or health-related establishment. I want to be as truthful as I can, and not remembering that day poses a problem for me, because I suppose I might have taken something. I just know from past experience that I was conscious of my body and health, and taking an illegal substance to enhance performance wasn't something I did.

Ezekiel 25:17, my investigator, and God himself had known that there was no reason Matthew 7:15 had any right to use his dog, which was most likely the cause of my fall, the moment he "feared" for his life. When the dog exited the squad car and was let off its leash, excessive "use of force" issues were at play. I was never commanded to stop; I was never told I was under arrest. I committed no crime. I was not a threat to anyone. I struggle with knowing that my case was thrown out and Duluth officials defended themselves successfully.

It's interesting to know that I was claimed to have been "fleeing" the police. I did nothing wrong, except maybe wanting nothing to do with Matthew 7:15. In his report, he said that at no time did he make any verbal announcements of his presence. He also admitted never using sirens or lights. Why was I placed in harm's way? Oh yeah, because I tried to avoid Matthew 7:15, at which point he used "excessive force" on a young man walking home from a party, intoxicated, committing no crime, and hurting nobody.

Makes perfect sense, doesn't it? It is heartbreaking when those who are supposed to protect you turn out to be, in reality, your greatest threat. We hear stories everyday about how our abusive system discriminates against those without power simply because…because of their skin color, because of their beliefs, or because they aren't twenty-one yet.

As the key inquiry regarding the use of the dog unfolded, I was indisputably turned into a felon, an addict, and a criminal all at once. It really was a shame that the attitudes towards others that we are required to follow under our divine law were abandoned. Ideals such as integrity, compassion, and heart were not part of Duluth's side of this story. God's word was forgotten there.

These were the basics of the case that was ultimately thrown out. Right away, I was mad of course; I was disgusted by the unfairness of our world. But then I realized that our world is not fair, and never will be. On the other hand, it is fair that I am given this opportunity to publish my story and shed light onto the problems involved in such an injustice.

When the case was first thrown out, I was beside myself. I never thought, with everything we knew, we'd ever lose. My perception of the hierarchy in the United States court system has changed. This initial defeat led us onto the state's Court of Appeals. We only went further because we couldn't, morally speaking, back down without giving our all to our cause in seeking justice.

The facts of that night were pretty obvious. Matthew 7:15 observed "non-criminal behavior" on my part. I was simply walking home, not wanting any more business with police officers for the remainder of the night. Then, on an "investigatory stop," an "unleashed dog" was dispatched; the dog was let out of the squad, and ran off. Keep in mind that the dog took off running without a command. What is difficult to understand is that Matthew 7:15 said his dog was "controllable." Did he or did he not give a command? Was the dog controllable or not? In the end, Matthew 7:15's dog probably drove me off the cliff as I was trying to escape its vicious bite.

The injuries on my right arm were consistent with a dog bite. As I said before, St. Luke's knew nothing of a dog's involvement. My family said that the nurses were treating wounds on my right wrist. If they had known a dog was involved, they might have been able to clarify whether or not the wounds were from the dog or from the fall.

According to a retired Los Angeles County deputy sheriff who served as our expert on police dog training protocol, the injuries on my right arm were "consistent" with training intended, "to bite the arms of a target and the defensive posture of a person fending off a dog attack." Yes, I am right arm dominant; I would have instinctively tried using my right arm to defend myself.

We discovered that Matthew 7:15's dog had made unprovoked attacks on others, a fact supporting the dog's "uncontrollability." One attack was on Matthew 7:15's own child, and another on the dog's kennel keeper. These incidents supported "control issues" regarding the integrity of the dog; it shouldn't, in fact, have been accompanying Matthew 7:15. Apparently Matthew 7:15 spoke with the kennel owner about the problems he was having with his partner, a disobedient canine. He didn't take to heart what the kennel owner had told him, and the dog continued its uncontrollable behavior.

Then, Matthew 7:15's "sensitivity to human life" came under review. Were his actions acceptable practices in fulfilling his duty as a police officer? Duluth's "use-of-force" policy was not adhered to; he was following his own policies in the matter. Finally, the court examined whether or not he gave misinformation about what actually happened. In other words, we tried to see if, how, and why he told a couple of fibs to cover his ass, and if he was credible: the future of a young Bulldog and the fate of a hostile beast-master were at the mercy of the courts. Unfortunately for us, the case didn't resolve in our favor.

I realize now that a positive attitude about this case, of course, would prevail. My anger and lack of faith concerning our society would transform back into one of optimism and trust. It didn't matter that my lawsuit never did for me what I had expected, that is, make me financially comfortable. Having a life is not about getting rich through the faults of a not-so-nice municipality; it is through the personal relationships you build and the trust you place in yourself and others.

And, as people read my story, I can lay to rest any false demons trying to challenge my view of what really happened during my most difficult, yet triumphant trial. In fact, this began the moment I began forgiving and, at the same time, began writing the first word of this book. The lawsuit in itself is irrelevant. Our winning wouldn't have changed what happened. It sure as hell wouldn't have changed the past.

In the end, we sued the city of Duluth and lost. So what? This in itself wasn't going to make my brain injury disappear or function any better. So it really didn't matter whether or not the dog and I faced each other. At first, this was difficult for me to accept. Of course, it was here that I once again recognized the most fundamental rule of life we must all accept: life will never be fair. This was just one moment, challenging me to decide how I would react: I could define the moment, or let the moment define me.

Ultimately, after about five years of waiting impatiently for our trial to conclude, the Minnesota Court of Appeals offered sympathy to me and my family about my experience. However, they granted summary judgment in favor of Duluth and that was it. Our luck had disappeared. I had thought that everything was lining up perfectly, that our suit would prove Duluth negligent, and we would win. It didn't matter that every opinion we sought said it would be damn near impossible to defeat an entire city. But then again, the "universe is unfolding as it should," right?

"Although waiting is not having, it is also [a kind of] having. The fact that we wait for something shows that in some way we already possess it."

(Kushner 2003)

SIX

Matters of the Heart

Let us consider everything I have endured. My walk home. The thirty-five-foot fall. The near drowning. My rescue. St. Luke's. Sister Kenny. Our lawsuit. Everything. How was this supposed to strengthen me? I could try to see how, or, I could refuse to see how. When I consider everything from my experience in Duluth, to my rehab at Sister Kenny, to attending Normandale Community College, to graduating from the University of St. Thomas, to working at Methodist Hospital, I have no choice but to see everything I've gained.

How did I manage it? I relied on my "inner" strength, my mind, to drive me. I was forced to take a good look at myself. I could be upset at the world, pissed off at whomever, disappointed in myself, but really, what the hell would that accomplish? Absolutely nothing. That's right... nothing.

A life is built on defining moments and self-will. I had to be methodical about this, working one inch at a time. Beating the odds, doing the impossible, or simply winning the game would be impossible without struggle and effort.

Consider the lives of Larry Bird and Michael Jordan, and every critic who said they weren't good enough to play basketball, or every person who said they would never dominate in a sport that required speed, agility, and more importantly, drive. That was the title of Larry Bird's book, *Drive*, in which he describes his journey toward becoming one of the greatest players of all time. The description on the inside jacket of his book says, "It's about overcoming obstacles by the sheer force of fierce determination and all-out hard work. It is this discipline, this work ethic—this drive—that make Larry Bird who he is: a real-life American hero." And he supposedly didn't have the ability. It's amazing to think how both men depended on the strength of their characters and how they dominated a sport that wasn't supposed to be their game.

It is in such conditions that individuals are defined. When I thought about writing my story, I had my doubts. I was used to writing five-page papers for school, not a two hundred-plus page memoir. However, as I have said before, writing is a great way for me to find "Nick" again and deal with a few of my meandering demons. Like I said, I was doubtful. Nevertheless, I continued to write, refining my words, but I really wasn't sure I could do it.

I was given so many signs that encouraged the possibility of *23*. One of the first signs was receiving a *Winner's Minute* written by probably the most charismatic pastor of my time, Mac Hammond. It was a *Winner's Minute* that would ultimately change my life, encouraging me to persevere and persist. Hammond wrote,

"Perseverance is all too rare a commodity these days. Theodore Giesel's first children's book was rejected by twenty-three publishers. The 24th publisher sold six million copies. Years later, "Dr. Seuss" died knowing his perseverance resulted in entertaining and educating millions of children.

"The value of perseverance is highlighted in many places in the bible. For example, Galatians 6:9 says, "And let us not be weary in well doing: for in due season we shall reap, if we faint not." Persistence is a vital quality for leaders today.

"My question for you is, 'Are you being tempted to quit where you need to persevere?'"

Can you imagine that? Being rejected by "twenty-three" publishers, only to have the twenty-fourth one make his work legendary. As God is my witness, and just as Dr. Seuss struggled to make his work known, 23 signifies hope, heart, and an undying spirit that perseveres despite the past. It challenges the seeming impossibilities of today. The heart will overcome; my number will define its victory.

As you have noticed, I like to compare myself to others who have persevered and realized their true virtues. Look at Dave Pelzer, someone who, in the midst of insanity, accepted his fate, did everything possible to live a more fruitful life, all the while focusing on strength, love, and determination. Pelzer inspires us to simply live for this moment as well as future ones. I have read all of his books and thought long and hard about them. Pelzer represents everything I believe in when it comes to persevering. I just needed to apply the same standards to my own life.

Being able to develop my character is the greatest gift I received after I was first forced to walk my path. So I had to stray off my course a little. So what? I had the ability to go back to college and finish what I started. I realized that college was never about getting a degree in business, or whatever the hell I studied in Duluth. It was never about that. I think about how I overcame all that was against me in my pursuit for a degree. Fatigue. A fragile memory. Weak executive skills. My difficulties changed me. And I embraced everything, strengthened my passion, and shaped who I wanted to be.

I now don't judge my success by what kind of job I have or how much money I make. It's a joke; and that dollar sign was my primary influence as I was studying business and management in Duluth. The world, as we see it, is so focused on making money that we have lost our core values and abandoned our principles and everything we stand for. It's almost sick how people trade their integrity and their faith for a few extra dollars.

Yeah, money is necessary to live and to participate in society, but when it is traded for values and ethics, it loses its moral worth. It shouldn't be used to jeopardize one's soul or one's respect towards eternity. Chasing and accumulating money is a lousy way of keeping score and there are always going to be others who make more money and there are always going to be those who resent them for it. I guess I am trying to say don't let money run your life. Do not become its prisoner. There are so many things that should come first: your family, your friends, and your personal relationships. Integrity. The list continues…

Life is not easy; and for me, it is a never-ending process meant to teach and serve. I am here to show the world that there is a road of hope, that recovery is possible, even when the so-called "experts" say it's not. It's a matter of having the right heart and believing in yourself and eliminating any possibility of becoming disillusioned. I needed to embody my strengthened heart, especially when things weren't going exactly as I planned.

Fighting for my life at St. Luke's led many into the arms of the Lord and His protection. From what I gather, there were people praying for me all over the United States. Fear was everywhere, in the eyes of the doctors, my parents, my family, and my friends. But I would not succumb to this fear. My life and my future were at stake. It wasn't going to be decided in a hospital room in Duluth by a select few skeptics or non-believers, or those who followed a "be realistic" attitude. That I couldn't allow, and neither could God.

The world meets nobody half way; if you want something, you have to take it. And living is always about believing, about letting no one undermine your dreams and lead you astray. Listen to someone who learned the hard way; be open to every possibility. I was prepared to get a degree in business, simply because that was all I knew. I didn't listen to my heart, and worst of all, I had to almost die to realize that.

People stay in jobs they hate and relationships that aren't good for them because of low self-esteem or the fact that they don't realize there is more out there. Believe me, there is more than you can possibly imagine. You just need to look past your initial perceptions when tragedy presents itself and you are faced with overwhelming challenges.

I always seemed to let things appear more important than they really were. Isn't that sad? I have been doing this forever, acting as if a current situation is a matter of life or death. After the trials and hardships are over, you realize that it actually wasn't as bad as you imagined and the difficulty was manageable. I have had times when my self-esteem wasn't where it should've been and I'd tell myself that I wasn't able to do what was in front of me since I had a disability. In reality, it was just a pathetic story I told myself because believing in the story was easy.

It is important never to sell yourself out, or bitch about how hard life is or how meeting a challenge can't be done. Focus on your abilities, what you can do. Not backing down is a victory in itself. There are so many people who quit when the first sign of adversity appears. It is when you are faced with insurmountable odds and the world is against you that you need to stop feeling sorry for yourself and decide to stand up.

Will you be alive? Or will you act dead? Never put your happiness in someone else's hands. Begin moving forward. Follow your path. Forget about the cowards, forget about the negatives, forget the disbelief, and forget about the self-doubt. Remember, anything is possible.

Dr. Phil wrote about the tragedy this world would have known had Einstein remained as a common merchant or a sailor. It is amazing the things we wouldn't have realized if Einstein hadn't decided to search for something more. It is in this search for something beyond our comfort levels where greatness is pioneered into reality. My choice to write was my obvious challenge.

I could have either continued feeling bitter about my life, focusing on how unfair it was, or I could change my attitude and accept my future. Yes, that's it. Attitude was the deciding factor. It can change your life, for better or worse. What if Elvis had continued to keep trucking without following his heart to be a performer, or Mother Teresa remained in a common profession? The potential we have in our hearts is something that cannot be questioned, and is, by far, the strongest feeling we'll ever know.

Being strong in mind involves having passionate energy, which helps greatness surface and fear subside. When I faced reality, when I had to choose between living or dying, my heart told me to choose life. Yes, I was unconscious, but I haven't doubted for one second that at that moment God spoke to me through my heart. He said that it was going to be a long, difficult journey, and there would be moments of pain, doubt, and overwhelming struggle. It would not be easy. At that point, I was given a moment of grace and then confronted God's will. I became stoic and determined.

Dr. Phil warns against mediocrity and advocates living purposefully. It is a reminder to never give in to criticism or self-doubt. Going through life trying not to lose serves no good purpose. This is my biggest fear, and strongest adversary: playing it safe. Of course, failure and disappointment always exist. But that should never discourage you from working incredibly hard, or steering away from going for it. The only thing worth focusing on is triumph, proving to yourself that there is nothing in this world you are incapable of achieving.

Dr. Phil exclaims, "When chores, routine existence, and just playing it safe become the only purpose in life, there is no purpose, and one must be found. You need to know your 'highest and best use' in this world, and then pursue it." Prior to my accident, I was prisoner to the mundane routines of following an ordinary existence. I saw only what was in front of me. I had sold myself out.

I wasn't focused. I didn't believe in myself. I tried too hard to please others. I was living without passion; then I met Matthew 7:15. The piece of advice I found to be most helpful was the recommendation by Dr. Phil to never beat yourself up. He writes, "Bottom line: It's bad enough if negative things happen in your life, but it becomes disastrous if they result in your kicking your own ass, making them worse." Damn, this is exactly what I had been doing; I kept weakening my self-confidence by kicking my own ass.

Limit your own self-abuse. In my case, it came down to never having enough confidence in myself to take a chance. This was no way to live, believe me. I think I have gotten to a point in my life where I do finally believe in myself. I mean seriously, if overcoming a near-death experience isn't enough of a kick in the ass for me, what the hell is? I walked "through the valley of the shadow of death"; I experienced the worst. If that time in my life didn't make me a true believer in myself, then nothing would.

Another piece of advice I found inspiring involves taking responsibility for things I had no control over. Dr. Phil writes, "There are enough things for which you are clearly and undeniably responsible without you taking on things over which you have no control." Time after time, I have felt that this entire event that changed my life was entirely my fault. I figured I was drinking. In fact, I figured I was drunk off my ass and this resulted in my fall. I had been at the party and knew right away, I was drunk. I knew right away that I was not making the right choice.

I take full responsibility for that, for my intoxication. But I am not the reason for my fall on a night when my life was placed in the hands of Matthew 7:15 and his canine partner. Given my memory loss and Matthew 7:15's questionable stories about that night, I may never know who was responsible for what.

So, as life goes on, I have dealt with my past and my life as best I can. This definitely was a matter of the heart. Dr. Phil is right when he says, "Your life has a root core that, once understood, unlocks a powerful force to create your life the way it was meant to be, the way you want and need it to be."

Focus is the key. And when you define your focus, a powerful force is unleashed and you will discover things you hadn't even known existed. Keep your heart centered and your spirits high. The rest will be history.

"It is almost impossible to feel powerless over your situation when you are helping another."

(Strand 2003)

SEVEN

Tough Love

Forgiveness cleansed me of all negativity and lessened the self-incrimination. For a long time, I was consumed with anger against myself and Matthew 7:15 after I learned the cycle of events that led to my accident. I blamed Matthew 7:15; there was no way in hell I was feeling so miserable because of something I did. God forbid I take responsibility for anything I did to make my life a living hell. It took me a long time to realize that there are always two sides, and part of the responsibility was, in fact, mine.

Blame is mostly and usually passed from one person to another. Society is consumed by accusations that so-and-so is responsible for causing this or doing that. Why can't we take responsibility for our actions instead of making accusations? It's just another one of the many problems we use as an excuse to heighten our level of self-esteem. There are no excuses. I wanted nothing more than for Matthew 7:15 to face the wrath of justice. I hoped he would lose his job, be abandoned by his family, and feel demoralized in front of the police force. But that wasn't the case.

Forgiveness must be immediate, at least according to Rick Warren. And I think, deep down in my heart, I forgave right away. I didn't seek revenge; I didn't take matters into my own hands; I sat back and let Ezekiel 25:17 bravely pursue justice.

Martin Luther King Jr. writes about loving your enemies as you would yourself. King writes, "It is also necessary to realize that the forgiving act must always be initiated by the person who has been wronged, the victim of some great hurt, the recipient of some tortuous injustice, the absorber of some terrible act of oppression." It was my responsibility to put this behind me, without hoping or praying that Matthew 7:15 got his. Yes, I would have loved for him to request forgiveness, but it first had to start with me. This is my responsibility, my debt to settle.

Knowing that I can never forget what happened, I cannot let it remain an obstruction to my fulfilling positive personal relationships, which is something I feel so strongly about. And if I don't do this, then this event has already beaten me, and that's nobody's fault but my own. King also writes, "There is some good in the worst of us and some evil in the best of us." I needed to know that Matthew 7:15 was human, and to have learned this from our encounter. And whether or not I actually hear the words "I'm sorry" from him, I must assume he is remorseful. When he radioed in the moment he froze, his morality surfaced and his humanity spoke for itself.

Recognizing this has definitely given me a broader perspective on life, which is just another benefit for me to add to the till. And it gave me this, my writing; the accident was the reason for this. So what if the police get away with acting like jackasses without paying the proper dues. That's reality. That's the truth. I am not the first person to get screwed, nor will I be the last. I wanted an apology; I guess I get this instead.

And who am I not to forgive this man? Who am I not to forgive myself, or my parents? I think Matthew 7:15 knew his dog was crazy, and did nothing. I've thought about trying to contact him, but something tells me to just let it go. Go forward.

So why did I have to experience the trauma that was caused, at least in part, by one of our shielded members of society? It must have just been my time to realize that pain and struggle are common, and that the joyride I was on doesn't last forever. I found out the truth. I found out what I was made of—both how strong I was and how vulnerable I was—and about the power of God. I was, in a sense, powerless in this situation. I was at the mercy of God and the remarkable capacity of my own ability to overcome nothing less than the impossible, where disadvantages were just obstacles to overcome.

Ann Landers wrote a heartfelt article on November 17th of 1999 describing the mindset necessary to discover your potential during difficult times. It is titled "Meant Well Parents" and in it, Ann offers the following advice and suggestions.

Ann Landers suggests that we, as young men and women starting our lives, need to move past the resentment we might feel about our parents having it so well. They have already experienced the difficulties we experience today and have hopefully reached the ever-so-nice tomorrows. And even though we may think we know what "real life" is, we will never have a clear-cut definition until we follow a day-by-day, live-or-die journey dealing with the unmistakably real life experiences that have already shaped our parents.

We need to value the lives of so many others who have paved our way. The Christopher Reeves, the Dave Pelzers, and the Trisha Meilis not only give us examples to turn to, they give us their hearts too. They show us that even though experts determined how their lives would turn out based simply on the probabilities of similar past cases, they chose to live their lives as spirited and purposeful journeys, where they were ultimately challenged while building what was meant to be their destinies. It was an article that will always have a place in my heart. Godspeed, Ann Landers.

My mom gave me this article that first year I was in rehab when I found myself depressed, frustrated, and bitter towards life. Ann Landers' writing opened my eyes to the life adversity brings and helped me realize the subtle truths adversity makes available. How true it is that we, as part of this younger generation, blame our parents for negatively influencing our lives. I was mad at my parents because I somehow felt it was their fault I was injured.

They had thought, at one time or another, that Duluth would be a great place for me. I was angry at them, despite loving them. What I didn't first recognize was that I had had many opportunities to transfer from Duluth, and I didn't. I didn't think I would have the same kinds of friendships at another college. But seriously, I see none of those so-called "many friends" I had when I was at school in Duluth. I see a previous teammate every now and then, but of those close friends I thought I had, they are nowhere to be seen.

They are living their lives as they had planned. They are married. They are doing God knows what, and to be completely honest, I could care less. With the exception of a select few, I don't care if I ever see any one of those "friends" I had in Duluth, ever again. They were part of my life then, but not now. Don't get me wrong; I wish them the best in all their pursuits. However, we are no more than acquaintances now.

And what the Ann Landers column taught me was that even though our lives might take completely different paths, our community with one another will endure. It is not that the people from my past will no longer have a place in my heart, just that we won't be sharing our lives together. Life will be happening for all of us and perhaps our roads will meet in the future once again.

Early on in my rehab, about the time I read Ann Landers' column, my speech was quite impaired, my physical characteristics altered, and my self-esteem destroyed. I have improved in every area, so much that I really don't consider them disabilities anymore. And I have met some pretty remarkable people who like me for me, who don't see the problems I see. My speech has improved considerably. My physical traits, well, I think I am in better shape now. My muscles are back to normal proportions, though my strength is still significantly impaired. I see my memory as slightly hindered when in reality it is stronger than ever.

What I once considered disabilities are now faded memories. Yeah, I have my difficulties; however, I can compensate for any trouble I now experience. This evolution I owe to my rehabilitation at Sister Kenny. My therapists helped me regain most of my skills and then some. It's truly a remarkable thing when you can transform someone like myself, who was pretty much dead weight, and produce the person I am today. That is quite an impressive representation of the abilities behind the Sister Kenny Institute. It was there that I began questioning why I felt it was necessary to push myself and work diligently towards a full recovery. And my recovery at Sister Kenny helped me move on to new challenges in my life, such as eventually attending St. Thomas.

After beginning my studies of ethics at St. Thomas, I soon began questioning the nature behind my suffering. Why was suffering necessary? Are there benefits? And if so, what are they? These age-old questions have kept even the most spiritual leaders in the dark. They are some of the most fundamental questions of our ever so peculiar existence in which we experience weak beliefs, weak morals, and face a future that remains uncertain.

I had posed my concern regarding my experience with suffering and that of many others to my professor, Bill McD., and he spoke simply of God's judgment and authority over our lives. Bill said it was about God willingly allowing these adversities, and sometimes tragedies, to occur in our lives without being the cause of them. I still struggle with this idea, so writing about it in my own words is somewhat difficult. I think I've had enough struggle to last a lifetime; writing about the way I view life now is supposed to be my way out of uncertainty.

I have become more acutely aware of how common traumatic brain injuries are. There are so many articles and so many stories about them. I am tired of hiding in the shadows, where my struggle is never seen. And I have lived too much of my life being a passive observer. Transformation in my case has been necessary, and this will only happen when I begin sharing myself with others. First off, I need to acknowledge that I have so much to offer. Secondly, I get along with everyone; it would be a shame for me to keep everything I've learned to myself. And finally, I have gained some valuable lessons concerning life, and since I have so much to give, it is my duty, my responsibility, to offer myself for the sake of others.

Searching for answers about my life from a spiritual perspective was central to my trying to make sense of my life. In trying to view things through God's eyes, I felt at ease with my life. Since everything God does is perfect, what I was experiencing, and the troubles I was having, were perfect. They were meant to shape me and guide me toward greater things.

Bill McD. also told me that God does not want us to suffer, and doesn't cause our pain, but rather allows it to happen to strengthen our hearts, characters, and faith. Bill McD. encouraged me to read an essay by Karl Rahner, titled "Why Does God Allow Us To Suffer?," in which Rahner supports this idea that God simply has to permit suffering, struggling, and death because of the "biological development of our species."

Suffering is just a characteristic of life; that is all it is. Suffering bring us closer to God and strengthens our relationship with Him. Struggling, on the other hand, has nothing to do with hurting or feeling the physical pain an individual who suffers feels. I have learned so much from the experience that should have killed me. When I consider everything, I find it difficult to even comprehend the magnitude of how many countless ways it has moved me in one direction versus another, provided me with certain choices while skipping others, and giving me the chance to change or maintain my attitude.

Reality, in my case, has been about tough love, about first losing myself to the unforgiving act of abandoning myself then taking responsibility for so much. Reality has been about meeting so many great people who have helped shape my personality, develop my passion, and give me ideas about life and what it entails. I was given the proper direction so I could find the man who so desperately needed to surface without being an ungrateful martyr. Going back to school was one necessary part of this discovery.

In going to St. Thomas, I learned the greatest lesson of all: having positive personal relationships helps define a successful life. It's not about the money or the status. Reality had been in my face, telling me I could never resume school and come back. Once again, I faced the choice to either remain in captivity and reach the point of taking my own life or, climb back up and finish what I had started in the company of others.

Personal experience is far more valuable than any degree or combination of degrees can offer. This is another reality. Keep this close to your heart, and never ignore the meaning behind the struggle or pain you experience. They are there for a reason. Consider what it has made of you, or has the potential to build within you as a fire that fuels your hunger. My will to succeed fed this hunger.

I had to eliminate all the blame associated with my shortcomings, while trying to see what level of responsibility I held myself. Struggling is part of life, and seeing the purpose this "tough love" offered clarifies in a single gesture of good faith what is required of you to overcome. And please remember the words of Ann Landers, "The same fire that melts butter can make steel strong." Your hardships will strengthen you. I know mine did.

"A better question would be 'Now that this has happened to me, what am going to do about it?'"

(Kushner 2001)

EIGHT

Courage Without Fear

Song of Courage

From the dissonant sound of fear within me,
I turn to you, O God of perfect harmony.
　　I have not felt like singing in a long time.
　　How I wish I did!
I remember when music filled my days,
sending me on my way inspired,
ready to meet any challenge.
　　I long to hear the music again.
O Lord who makes trembling hearts brave,
attune the ears of my spirit
to your eternal refrain of courage.
　　Renew my trust that those refrains never end,
　　that they play on
　　in spite of grief's efforts to silence them.
May I listen now.

So many fears assail me.
I lie awake at night worrying
about my finances, my family, my future.
I have fears about my health, my job, my relationships.
Sometimes I feel that my fears are driving me insane!
Let me not believe that I can be brave on my own.
Remind me that courage is a gift of your grace,
that I can't manufacture it, only surrender to it.
Turn my mourning into dancing as I hear
your song of courage and learn to sing it myself.
This is the melody that helps to mend a broken heart.
Do your work of mending now, O God,
and my lips will sound forth your praise. Amen.

—*Evan Howard*

Was this inevitable, incapable of being avoided or evaded? Was it bound to happen? My accident and recovery was necessary for the development of my soul. Without proper struggle, I would not progress. Some people deal with positives, such as a promotion or beginning a new life with a new partner. My experience involved neither. I advanced through a different passage, one full of struggle, pain, difficulties, and adversity. Perhaps my prosperous journey was similar to the sun trying to escape the barrier of a vicious storm.

My destiny was fulfilled. My progress began with a terror-filled situation as the starting point for my discovering my purpose. The Chinese view this type of voyage in the most profound way, formulated by the following equation:

Crisis = Danger + Opportunity

My tragic beginning, with all its negativity, soon evolved into unforeseen opportunity. Life can be extremely overwhelming, almost to the point where you'd rather not even try at all. Sometimes the things that should break you, exhausting everything you've got physically and mentally, can be the very things that offer such prosperity. We see this everyday, when people turn their failures into an abundance of success and victory. And we find out who we are and how strong we can be.

So, as we face danger, we find ourselves tapping into undiscovered resources within. This so-called danger is what helps us realize our potential, our willpower, and the power of our faith. Nobody knows how we are going to come out of something heartrending, in my case an event that should have left me broken for good. Nobody had any idea how strong my internal "self" truly was. My family and friends, in fact, were given a gruesome picture of my future, a picture that didn't leave much hope.

My future was uncertain. I would have surely died had my angels not saved me and the medics arrived when they did. This was the time when my faith needed to save me and my true strengths expressed. Why? Because this was when I was most vulnerable. God uses vulnerability and weakness in order to strengthen people. I don't really feel as though I was weak by any means when I was hospitalized; however, I was on the verge of death. Someone who was weak, who didn't have the tenacity of a bulldog, wouldn't have been able to endure this.

I admit I remember nothing of my hospital stay in Duluth, so I re-live it through stories and commentary of those who were there, those who saw me at my weakest moment. Or was it my strongest? People came together, praying for the future of a young Bulldog. Author Dr. James Dobson cites Kierkegaard, who best describes this kind of attitude: "Faith is holding onto uncertainties with passionate conviction." Without me, many hearts were in jeopardy, and despite the grim reports, there was no doubt in their minds that I would return in full.

My life, in the concluding months of 1998, was far from good. The road to achievement on which I had been walking was ripped out from under my feet as I was placed on a new path. There was no map or guide to follow, just my heart. I suppose if you follow your heart, you can never be wrong. Following your heart, is this ridiculous? Am I dreaming to think you can accomplish greatness simply by believing? Maybe. Hebrews 11:1, says, "Now faith is being sure of what we hope for and certain of what we do not see." Before my accident, I wouldn't have believed.

What did I need to be certain of? This is a little more difficult to interpret. My imagination needed to evolve for this to occur. Being certain of what I couldn't see was the key. 2 Corinthians 4:18 states this beautifully, saying, "So we fix our eyes not on what is seen, but on what is unseen. For what is seen is temporary, but what is unseen is eternal." I saw only my deficiencies; I saw that I could not walk, or had trouble speaking, or had no confidence. When I was going to therapy, when I was lacking understanding and faith, I focused on what I had lost, and on what I couldn't do. This didn't serve my purpose because I was so intent on looking at everything I had lost.

Even though I saw my therapists, nurses, and support staff everyday, I only saw them on the surface. I didn't recognize the relationships that were building, or my true appreciation of their service. I wouldn't be where I am today without them. I wouldn't have my passion for serving others, or serving humanity. This I can be sure of. I only saw what was visible from the narrow tunnel vision from which my brain injury allowed me to see.

However, after seven years, my field of vision has expanded, and I see things I was unable to see only a few years ago, including all that I've accomplished due to the power of my spirit. It is amazing what can be accomplished with the right mind-set and the right motivation, when accompanied by the right faith. Prior to my coming into this consciousness, I focused on the wrong desires, the wrong motivation. I had forgotten about everything Jesus taught and His image of service.

So many times our focus is askew; mine was off center. I walked through life with my eyes fixed on something that didn't fit into my basic worldview. Remember, changing my focus really wasn't that difficult. Like most things, it always seems harder than it really is.

But in reality, it is simply not that terrifying to the person with the courage to take that first step towards a new way of living. It is much easier than expected. Isn't this the truth with almost everything? I used to get so bent out of shape over meaningless obstacles: exams, quizzes, papers, new jobs, new relationships, my image, money, even pain. And when facing them is over, it generally proves to be a hell of lot easier and less stressful than anticipated.

Everyone who supported me and everyone I met, read about, or discovered proved to be angels on my shoulders, protecting my every step. They have given me examples to follow, turning their attempts into works of genius. Many have been beaten down only to get back up.

I thank everyone who overcame adversity for being true examples of what it takes to endure, to overcome. I am, once again, forever indebted. You are the ones who have given me inspiration to accept my life. I have spent enough time feeling sorry for myself. My gratitude is the measure of my soul, and my soul must become perfectly harmonious.

Mac Hammond has given me much encouragement to deal with difficult times. Hammond strengthened my belief that there is a reason why chaos exists. It is not God testing us, but rather the scrutinizing of our faith and what we believe.

In *Enduring Adversity*, Hammond defines a test as, "a putting to proof by experience of adversity." The proof of my faith was the result of the test of my challenges.

It takes a strong person to endure life's battles and I can't stress enough the importance of mental toughness. This is what gets most people over the hurdles of daily living. Hammond suggests, "never make a decision to relieve the pressure that adversity brings," whether it be financial, surgical, or whatever. I learned to embrace my adversity.

Life is, as we know it, about serving others and serving our conscience. It's taken me twenty-seven years, which I feel is short in comparison to a lifetime, to realize this. I am still young; many don't realize their purposes until later in life. I was fortunate to learn mine when I still had time to change my focus, my motivation, and my ambition.

One of my favorite phrases that offered me inspiration, courage, and drive in recognizing my purpose was Yoda's wisdom from *Star Wars*, a film produced by George Lucas. Yoda's most meaningful suggestion is,

"Try not. Do. Or do not. There is no try."

I could try all I wanted, only to find myself still struggling, still fighting, and still searching. I had to really commit to doing what was needed to excel. Read each word carefully, and apply it to your life. This suggestion Yoda offers can be applied to any life, so don't assume it is just for sci-fi fans. I could apply Yoda's advice to my life and my struggle for my true self.

I remember back in high school when I was struggling to feel confident in my abilities and be a good enough athlete. My dad had written down those exact words of Yoda. It really put athletic ability into perspective as I soon realized the importance of a mentally tough attitude where it was more about heart and desire than size and natural ability.

Norman Vincent Peale writes about enduring difficulties, questioning our sense of worth, and having a successful attitude:

"Are you going to crawl through life on your hands and knees, piteously saying how difficult everything is? Take a long look at the potential that the Almighty God has built into you. You will discover that you can do tremendous things with yourself. You will discover that you can find true meaning in life, real personal inner organization."

I had to retrain my thinking. It is one thing to be focused, but it is another thing to be totally engrossed in your cause, purpose, personal relationships, and service. Believe in the inevitability of your glory and the reality behind unforeseen opportunities. I had to take that long look Peale suggested.

Yoda says, and my dad said to me back in high school, that "There is no try"; you either do it or you don't. Don't miss the power behind this verse. This can be applied to everything we set out to accomplish: getting a job, reaching fitness goals, pursuing an education. Accomplishing such goals requires dedication, heart, but most of all, not giving up too soon. When you take one step, you will be closer to reaching your destination on your next attempt. So do not give up...ever. Just do it. And let us not forget the inspiration of Christopher Reeve, who wrote,

"The future does not belong to those who are content with today, apathetic toward common problems and their fellow man alike, timid and fearful in the face of bold projects and new ideas. Rather, it will belong to those who can blend passion, reason and courage in a personal commitment to the great enterprises and ideals of American society."

I now see that it was inevitable that I would overcome. As human beings, we are all inherently challenged to be the best we can possibly be; anything less would lack meaning. When my body was broken it seemed that defeat was near. However, underneath that facade, a life was struggling, a new birth was beginning.

And in a poster I received that first Christmas post-TBI was a quotation from Theodore Roosevelt, who is known for distinguishing perseverance from fear that offers the following advice:

"The credit belongs to those people who are actually in the arena, who know the great enthusiasms, the great devotions to a worthy cause. Who at best, know the triumph of high achievement; and who at worst, fail while daring greatly...so that their place shall never be with those cold and timid souls who know neither victory nor defeat."

"It is only when we are faced with death that we gain the vision of life."

(Michelle Saari, friend)

"Once you learn how to die, you learn how to live."

(Albom 1997)

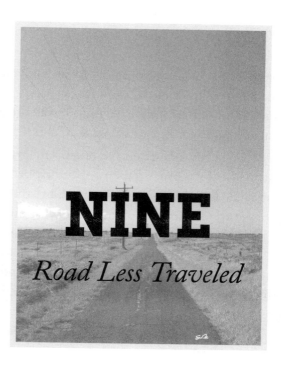

NINE

Road Less Traveled

"*The Sister Kenny Institute Coma Assessment Program provides multidisciplinary assessment and planning for patients in coma. This is a short stay program of approximately 2-3 weeks. At the conclusion of the program, individualized recommendations are provided relating to patient care, positioning, on-going rehabilitation, and follow-up*" (Sister Kenny assessment). October 15th was the start of my rehabilitation, a day when I was unconscious, in a coma, struggling for my very existence.

Imagine being confined to a wheelchair, almost frozen in time, enduring necessary rehabilitation, making that effort, every day, to learn how to do things all over again. I wasn't given very much leeway about whether or not I wanted to make it back: my nurses and doctors just began my rehab program. At first, I was incompetent; I had no idea what the hell was going on. I was vulnerable; I was weak. I pretty much just went along with whatever everybody else told me. My brain was still healing; I was unable to do much physically, and worse, I was unable to think for myself.

When I first began my extensive rehab, my grandpa Jack would be at the hospital every day so I wouldn't be alone until my mom arrived. It was during that first Christmas of 1998 that he gave me the Bible he took overseas with him in 1950. It was an emotional gift that I didn't fully appreciate until years later. However, I did at first bookmark Psalm 23 for quick reference as that passage took on new meaning in my life after this adversity. Grandpa's gift to me restored my soul; it was part of my destiny.

During rehab, my brain was rewiring signals and paths at a pace of astronomical proportions. I was relearning the skills necessary to speak and write and develop the fine motor skills necessary for me to live my life productively. At this point in my life, I required a lot of help, on all levels, physically and mentally. As an athlete, I found physical therapy the most enjoyable. And of course, it was the first to go. Occupational therapy was the biggest pain in my ass, so it lasted. And speech therapy, well, I still have trouble defining my most devious opponent.

I had a few problems with my speech before my accident, and really, this wasn't new to me. In the past, I had been ridiculed for not talking normally or for talking funny. Such moments produced feelings of helplessness. The first time was when I was a sophomore in high school, and then again, shortly after I was released from in-patient rehabilitation at Sister Kenny. Reminiscing on my past hurts reminded me of a quotation from Eleanor Roosevelt my friend Tricia offered me that solidified my past level of confidence: "Nobody can make you feel inferior without your consent." That was it. Because I was fearful, I allowed both experiences to make me feel inferior.

I don't remember my first sessions in speech therapy. I was too much in my own little world, too numb to recognize all that was happening. I was wheelchair-bound during those early sessions, and was living at the hospital. My memories of the encounters are so vague that I have a difficult time remembering anything.

My mom was with me as I met with Susan, my first speech therapist, and has helped me remember the early days. Much of it is really amazing to me, and I often would rather not recall myself in such a state. It can be humbling and rather humorous, though. Mom wrote the following: "In speech therapy they are working on getting you to use your mouth again. Yesterday Susan wanted you to stick out your tongue at her. You wouldn't do it for her but when she left the room I asked you to stick your tongue out at me and you did! I was thrilled." I guess my past behavior remained, since I had always been more comfortable with family and would never have wanted to offend anyone.

The most memorable activity during those early therapies with Susan was my swallow evaluations. These were done to test the capacity of my throat to deal with volatile, thin liquids. I remember attempting to swallow some Mountain Dew and choking. I also recall doing a little work on my memory, and retrieving simple ideas. We had to start easy.

My mom also wrote about the strength of my convictions and how much progress I was making. She wrote, "Your voice is weak right now but you even answer questions for us. It is so wonderful to hear your voice again. I told you, I Love You, and you answered back, I Love You, too! It was the 'too' that got to me because I knew you weren't just repeating me."

My short-term memory was barely working, and since I was in rough shape, it's amazing that I remember some aspects of what early rehab was like; reading Mom's journal brought back a lot of good memories. I eventually graduated to the next level of speech, and got a new therapist, Debbie, who offered me an entirely new perspective. I again worked mostly on memory skills, like retrieving and storing simple ideas, which confused me, since I thought I was supposed to be doing speech therapy. I wanted to focus on talking, not everything but talking. I think it was then that I began to realize the severity of my disabilities and the importance of my mind. My early speech therapies were somewhat of a preparation for what I was about to experience next, this time with someone who would change my life forever.

After being released from therapy, I felt my speech needed a little more work, so I scheduled an appointment to meet with Dr. Anita L. Kozan, a speech and language pathologist. Her office was decorated beautifully, a reflection of her commitment to her patient's comfort. She had two comfortable chairs next to a shelf with a stereo, away from her desk. Anita was all about relaxation. The lights were dimmed softly to enhance the atmosphere. I learned so much from her, not only about speech, but about life itself. She taught me fundamentals behind being a morally upright young man with a strong purpose.

A favorite idea I heard during our time together was one that sums up my entire journey wonderfully: the universe is unfolding as it should. How true is that? This basically implied that my experience, my TBI, was part of the entire plan from the beginning. It happened at exactly the right moment, and my recovery was done at exactly the right pace. What more could I ask for? My recovery rate was phenomenal. My rehabilitation and my life were unfolding in proportion to the precision developed under God's supervision.

Anita taught me about personal issues, such as proper etiquette and how sometimes first impressions aren't necessarily right. Her crazy blonde hair still amazes me to this day. Sometimes, when you meet someone so remarkable, you don't realize that they possess the power to take away pains and sorrows you thought would never fade.

My time with her was nothing less than extraordinary. When I requested more speech therapy, I had figured it would be a lot of pronunciation and practice on my part. I was wrong again. It was more like going to school, where I would have reading assignments, writing assignments, with some actual speaking requirements. I guess I had a lot to learn about speech communication, since I read that 80 percent of communication is attitude and body language; only 20 percent is verbal. In fact, it is probably less than that. My impressions about my speech weren't accurate; I had initially hoped to work on my actual speaking skills, but what I really got was a preliminary course in how to live successfully.

I learned about maintaining personal relationships with others and the importance of building bridges instead of walls. Anita showed me the value of friendship and the importance of being true to yourself. We still keep in touch, and I hope to have her in my life forever. She has left footprints on my heart. Her attitude towards me, and our ability to connect, was deep and reflective. I progressed in leaps and bounds after our work began.

She was comfortable enough to share some of her personal life experiences with me, and I also shared with her. After we disclosed parts of our lives with one another, I knew I had met a friend for life. Anita has proven to me her level of commitment to helping others, much like those adversity-bearers I previously mentioned, and I am forever blessed. I can't imagine not having her in my life.

Since I had always been a physical person who focused on vitality and athleticism, applying myself in the mental aspect of occupational therapy was something of a burden. School, both high school and college, had always been an automatic success for me. Hard work had been ingrained into my psyche since about the fifth grade, when I brought home a poor report card.

But I had a hard time seeing the benefits of OT. I fought it at first, not wanting to apply myself wholeheartedly, especially since I hadn't yet become as physically strong as I wanted to be. I didn't push myself hard enough, like when I was required to make phone calls to businesses and people I didn't know and who didn't know me.

My speech wasn't clear and I honestly just didn't want to sound like a fool, even though I didn't really care what the person on the other end of the line thought of me. It was difficult; it all seemed trivial to me. Shopping for groceries in a make believe store seemed childish; it felt like I was playing house and not acting my age. I had to assemble a doormat. I couldn't, for the life of me, see the reason for that. What a bunch of stupid tasks. Or were they?

I couldn't see the benefits of OT. But as we soon realize, as the film *Big Fish* suggests, the "more difficult something is, the more rewarding it will be in the end." The things I was unable to appreciate while enduring OT have proven invaluable, as they were rooted in the everyday tasks of daily living. Luckily, I saw the benefit before it was too late. I eventually saw that it would get me ready to live a more productive life once I had learned some invaluable lessons.

My first job post-TBI, which I began while I was enduring my outpatient rehab at Sister Kenny, promoted the progress of my occupational skills. It was working as an executive assistant for the corporate office of my father's business. Here I regained some interpersonal skills by answering phones and strengthened organizational skills through surveying customers, doing mailings, and filing the comprehensive cash report.

I owe a lot of my progress to those I saw everyday at this job. Tom, Dave, Ken, Sharon, Mike, Jim, and Ron gave me the opportunity to strengthen my skills, and were patient with the speed of my learning. Sharon taught me the fundamentals behind all the tasks I would be responsible for; her soft enduring nature proved encouraging. I am especially grateful for her part in tying up all the loose ends I most likely left behind.

Physical therapy was fun; it was like gym class. At first, I was unable to walk, and required a wheelchair. I wanted to walk, but every time I tried, I would fall flat on my ass. I quickly realized not to be ungrateful for the privilege of walking ever again. So I was in a wheelchair, most often pushed by someone else because I wasn't strong enough or didn't have the coordination to maneuver it. I usually applied myself without too much coaxing in PT. Friedrich Nietzsche said it best: "He who would learn to fly one day must first learn to stand and walk and run and climb and dance; one cannot fly into flying." Nietzsche summed up my PT experience perfectly. In all honesty, I just wanted to fly into flying, not having the patience to rebuild myself one brick at a time.

I really struggled with balance; my equilibrium was off. I struggled with everything from walking a straight line to getting myself up from the floor. It wasn't long before I recognized how fortunate I truly was to still be able to walk. Demons will always be a part of your life; however, like I have said before, your attitude is your best ally.

An email I received early on in my recovery opened my eyes to the glory behind my struggle for self. It is called "The Story of Life," and it is an inspiring, motivational reading that can change your perspective. Hopefully you will enjoy it as much as I have. Read on...

THE STORY OF LIFE

Sometimes people come into your life and you know right away that they were meant to be there to serve some sort of purpose, teach you a lesson, or to help you figure out who you are or who you want to become. You never know who these people may be (possibly your roommate, neighbor, coworker, long lost friend, lover, or even a complete stranger).

But when you lock eyes with them, you know at that very moment they will affect your life in some profound way.

And sometimes things happen to you that may seem horrible, painful, and unfair at first, but in reflection you find that without overcoming those obstacles you would have never realized your potential, strength, willpower, or heart.

Everything happens for a reason.

Nothing happens by chance or by means of good luck.

Illness, injury, love, lost moments of true greatness, and sheer stupidity all occur to test the limits of your soul. Without these small tests, whatever they may be, life would be like a smoothly paved, straight, flat road to nowhere. It would be safe and comfortable, but dull and utterly pointless.

The people you meet who affect your life, and the success and downfalls you experience, help to create who you are and who you become.

Even the bad experiences can be learned from.

In fact, they are probably the most poignant and important ones. If someone hurts you, betrays you, or breaks your heart, forgive them, for they have helped you learn about trust and the importance of being cautious when you open your heart.

If someone loves you, love them back unconditionally, not only because they love you, but because in a way, they are teaching you to love and how to open your heart and eyes to things.

Make every day count.

Appreciate every moment and take from those moments everything that you possibly can for you may never be able to experience it again. Talk to people that you have never talked to before, and actually listen.

Let yourself fall in love, break free, and set your sights high. Hold your head up because you have every right to. Tell yourself you are a great individual and believe in yourself, for if you don't believe in yourself, it will be hard for others to believe in you. You can make of your life anything you wish. Create your own life and then go out and live it with absolutely no regrets.

Most importantly, if you LOVE someone tell him or her for you never know what tomorrow may have in store.

And learn a lesson in life each day that you live.

The more important phrases to remember are in bold type. Keep these in mind when meeting new people, and always know that those you meet, even under the most traumatizing circumstances, are there for a reason. Learn the lessons you're given and never hold back when times are tough; it is during these moments when your true self emerges.

Another message that offers a similar vision comes from a book called *The Language of Positive Thinking*. A close friend, Roberta, gave this book to me after I graduated college. She decided to give me something that I'd have forever and it addresses something I am passionate about, positive thinking. One passage in the book is called "Have Positive Thoughts, and Always 'Hang in There,'" by Douglas Pagels, and it offers the following advice:

> "Difficulties arise in the lives of us all. What is most important is dealing with the hard times, coping with the changes, and getting through to the other side where the sun is still shining just for you.
>
> "It takes a strong person to deal with tough times and difficult choices. But you are a strong person. It takes courage. But you possess the inner courage to see you through. It takes being an active participant in your life. But you are in the driver's seat, and you can determine the direction you want tomorrow to go in.
>
> "Hang in there…and take care to see that you don't lose sight of the one thing that is constant, beautiful, and true: Everything will be fine—and it will turn out that way because of the special kind of person you are.

"So…beginning today and lasting a lifetime through—hang in there, and don't be afraid to feel like the morning sun is shining…just for you."

(Pagels 1999)

This advice is exactly what I needed, and still need, especially when I feel like giving up or when I reflect on where I'd be had all this not happened. When I feel like giving up, I forget about everything I've gained. There was no reason why I should remain in the shadows, in the valley of the shadow of death, away from the sun. Remember, instead of focusing on what has been taken from you, try and see the reason behind its absence. It might turn out to be a blessing in disguise.

What resulted from a terrible experience provided me lessons I could use. Receiving the email containing "The Story of Life" during that first year I was rehabilitating myself gave me not only inspiration I could apply to my situation, it gave me an awareness that was priceless: we can learn from *even the bad experiences*. Yes, this "bad experience" that began as a heartbreaking moment turned into a mandatory course in the education of life. The gift from Douglas Pagels allowed me to realize that everyone deals with difficulties, not just me. And *"beginning today and lasting a lifetime through,"* my life and future will unfold as they should, being influenced positively by the hurts of my past.

"If we are strong, our strength will speak for itself. If we are weak, words will be no help."

(John F. Kennedy)

TEN

Moments to Search

More than Second Best

I come to you, O God of resurrection and renewal,
to reorient my thinking.
I have been idealizing the life I knew before my loss.
From the perspective of today,
yesterday looks so perfect,
a fantasy of fulfillment and abundance.
Then came the devastation that changed everything.
Now my possibilities seem so limited,
so mundane compared with what could have been.
Silence in me this worn-out lament
about how incomparable life used to be.
Speak to me instead about the growth and learning,
friendship and accomplishment, beauty and joy
that await me in times to come.

Inspire in me a creative response to life after loss,
that you and I together may fashion
a masterpiece from the ashes.
Guard me from seeing this life as second-best,
as if you offer only one chance at happiness,
and to miss it is never to regain it.
Anoint my soul with the oil of hope, dear Lord.
Then I will believe that the best is yet to be,
that I have only begun to discover the surprises
you have in store for me.
Open my heart to these surprises, O God,
that the resurrection life you want for me
will be mine at last. Amen.

—*Evan Howard*

Acknowledging the difficulties life presents us is crucial to living well. So many people have to endure the worst life has to offer, such as losing a child, getting cancer, having a stroke, or receiving a head injury. That's life; it's out of our hands. We travel our daily paths with fear and anxiety and there's nothing we can do about it. There are, however, certain things we can do to alleviate the stress. Find an activity and commit to it daily. Read. Exercise. Play sports. Compose music. Go to church. Volunteer. Do anything.

Remember that passage about positive thinking in the previous chapter? There are so many books and encouraging writings meant to inspire and motivate us as we walk in this world trying to keep our heads above water. One good thing about positive thinking is the way it encourages us to reflect on the past. I like to reflect on every event in which I was ridiculed or treated badly, and consider how I reacted. I often reacted inappropriately. I would think later, if only I would have said this, or done that, that would have made all the difference. We always regret the things we didn't do rather than appreciate the things we did. I don't want to look back always wondering why I let something as trivial as a lack of confidence hold me down. Positive thinking helps us see the best in things we've done.

It's funny how we always remember the bad experiences, where we were, what time of day it was, and who was involved. The really great times are often forgotten and the memories of them are hard to retrieve. It doesn't matter how many fabulous moments I've had, the negative ones always surface more easily. Regardless of unavoidable situations, moving beyond the past is necessary. It's over. I learned valuable lessons from this. Let it go.

Do not become a prisoner of your past. That's simple advice, but I've had a hard time letting go, and not allowing all the "what ifs" to control my life. What if I had transferred from Duluth before my accident? What if I hadn't gotten so drunk that night? What if Matthew 7:15 hadn't seen me? I often focus on every decision I didn't or shouldn't have made. I never should have tried so hard to avoid the officer. I should have done this; I shouldn't have done that. That's all water under the bridge. I've discovered a more suitable purpose, one in which worrying about what might have been becomes useless.

I exercise and weight train daily. I've finished college. I have written a book. It is hard to believe that, if I hadn't been harassed, I'd most likely be working in a business setting for some company, too focused on money, feeling unfulfilled, and out of step with my God-given purpose. God had different plans for me, and my accident was how He brought it to my attention.

I credit my triumphs to my personal relationships, my drive to succeed, my motivation to never give up, and enduring this burden, even if it was more than I thought I could bear. It's important to waste no time on what could have been. One of my favorite messages I have heard comes from the movie *Man Without a Face*, starring Mel Gibson. Gibson's character tells his young protégé, "The best is yet to be." Forget about failures. Forget about past defeats. The future is always something to hunger for. Keep in mind that the best is, of course, yet to be a reality in your life.

Defining moments are significant events that can potentially lead to positive or negative outcomes, simply based on how you react. When I was told to "talk normal" by one of my teammates in 1993 or was asked why I "talked funny" in 1999, I was given opportunities to meet individuals who were challenging me. It's impossible not to meet such challenging people, with so many people, and so many different personalities. I've realized that individuals can be cruel, and they may be obsessed with their politically correct or incorrect attitudes, and that people get hurt and are treated terribly.

We all know the phrase, "sticks and stones may break my bones, but words, they'll never hurt me." Forget that expression. Words can and do hurt. I think what hurt the most when I was treated badly by others was that I didn't have the confidence to stand up for myself. There have been times I should have defended myself, and I didn't. After such moments, such defining moments, I vowed I'd never hurt another person. My suggestion: be nice to everyone.

I discovered something online one day that fit my understanding of compassion. It is probably one of the most genuine writings I have ever read. It is a list of commandments. These directives are clear and can be applied immediately. They are the "Paradoxical Commandments," and were developed by Kent M. Keith, who wrote, *Do It Anyway: The Handbook for Finding Personal Meaning and Deep Happiness in a Crazy World*. After reading these commandments, I learned that they all contribute some enlightening idea that helped me see how to strengthen my personal relationships. His instructions are meaningful and deeply felt. Read on...

The Paradoxical Commandments

People are illogical, unreasonable, and self-centered.
Love them anyway.
If you do good, people will accuse you of selfish ulterior motives.
Do good anyway.
If you are successful, you win false friends and true enemies.
Succeed anyway.
The good you do today will be forgotten tomorrow.
Do good anyway.
Honesty and frankness make you vulnerable.
Be honest and frank anyway.
The biggest men and women with the biggest ideas can be shot down by the smallest men and women with the smallest minds.
Think big anyway.
People favor underdogs but follow only top dogs.
Fight for a few underdogs anyway.
What you spend years building may be destroyed overnight.
Build anyway.
People really need help but may attack you if you do help them.
Help people anyway.
Give the world the best you have and you'll get kicked in the teeth.
Give the world the best you have anyway.

©Kent M. Keith 1968, renewed 2001

The insights in Keith's commandments are incredible. The instructions for serving your purpose are quite simple. Loving thy neighbor is about the most undemanding task a person can follow. I harbor no ill will towards Matthew 7:15 or my critics; they are only human, and humans make mistakes. I make mistakes. It is all in the past.

The people I have met and the lessons I learned were given to me during difficult circumstances. Therefore, I am grateful I had the heart to endure. It is because of these experiences that I am who I am, and I am not who I'm not. I imagine where I'd be without them, and even though I might have had an easier time in high school and I'd be physically stronger and perhaps further along in my career development, I wouldn't have gained the level of compassion I now possess. How to develop a gentler soul is something I cannot fully explain; however, I feel its presence. Perhaps it's a phenomenon learned through experiences or one of God's miracles; time will tell.

When I think about the word "miracle," I think of the movie *Signs*, starring Mel Gibson and Joaquin Phoenix, which is about both characters' battles against aliens and personal demons. It is about how an individual, Gibson's character, a small town pastor who lost his faith after a life-altering event that took his wife, persevered. His relationship with God was challenged and the entire movie focuses on him finding his way back into God's arms.

At one point during the film, Gibson's character speaks to the character played by Phoenix and says, "See what you have to ask yourself is what kind of person are you? Are you the kind that sees signs, sees miracles? Or do you believe that people just get lucky? Or, look at the question this way: Is it possible that there are no coincidences?" Here, he challenged the idea that everything that happens and everything we experience is ordained by God and unfolds as it should.

Knowing that we are under His command, we feel all our anxiety evaporates. I am currently working as a nursing assistant at Methodist Hospital's ICU for a reason. God needed me to break the self-created prison I was in, and to appreciate fully the intense experience my family and friends went through in 1998. God wanted me to see the reality behind being so close to death. God saw my need to experience what those close to me felt and how my life could impact the world. I accepted such a responsibility.

Seeing struggle in its most primitive form helped me find myself. Being able to see the pain and struggle the ICU produces is probably what I was supposed to see, so I'd understand my past as completely as I could. I was unconscious at St. Luke's when I arrived in 1998. I was blind to the pain felt by so many. I needed to see it firsthand so I could understand what Duluth was all about. It hasn't been pretty. It has been intense; it has been severe. Coincidence? Absolutely not.

According to Keith, we are to do good regardless of anyone's opinion about our motive. Those in Duluth saw my lifeless body and took it upon themselves to bring me home faithfully. The doctors operated, the nurses kept me safe, and God defined my purpose, that of seeking the benefit of others. Our success is independent of those envious souls who feed off of our glory. Envious people are only here to feel worthy illegitimately through our accomplishments or failures. We ought to succeed without worrying about how our success influences another who may or may not be a true friend.

Good deeds should be done for the sake of serving, not for the recognition or the image. I was saved, not for the doctors' or nurses' glory, but for God's, so I could live with integrity. Living with integrity helps the soul develop. Leaving behind a legacy based on truth and honor ought never be jeopardized; it is forever. I am my own legacy and those who ridicule and demoralize others, like those who ridiculed me, are simply insecure about their own abilities.

What about everyone who has big ideas and strong urges to develop them but are sometimes discouraged by others to do so? Jealousy is often the cause. People are resentful and bitter at the expense of what someone else has achieved. But this is a ridiculous response. There is always going to be someone who has more money, a bigger house, better car, or just an easier life. We have enough problems and anxieties as it is; what someone else has should be of no concern. Kent suggests we ought to think big, without considering how others will react. Perhaps that's a reflection on me, on my writing. I need to think big—regardless of how self-conscious I am about putting myself out there for criticism.

My favorite commandment of Keith's says, "People favor underdogs but follow only top dogs. Fight for a few underdogs anyway." How common is that? I am guilty of it, and I would bet most everyone else is too. We always want the person or team who is the long shot to win, but we put our money on the other. Why is that? It's hard to believe in the underdog. As a result, we don't fight for that underdog with enough enthusiasm, enough passion. I was the underdog; death was almost a sure thing. Should I then assume there were those who never thought I'd make it back? It was after my dad asked the doctor if I had "a shot" that first day that my purpose slowly began to meet my future.

In the past, I would get so wrapped up in my own struggle that I'd lose sight of what was truly important. People spend years developing their careers or their image, just to fall victim to the sheer impact of great misfortune. People give years to building up their lives, but these lives can be destroyed in a matter of seconds. We see this everyday. Others work their entire life to get businesses up and running and then they are destroyed by a massive hurricane that demolishes everything in its path.

The same thing applies to building a reputation. Accusations are made, lies are told, and, as a result, an individual's character is tarnished. This is just what happened when Duluth news stories made me out to be an addict and a criminal. Even though others can defame you, give more of yourself to your reputation. It is all about respect, honor, and staying true to your principles. Our world relies on those willing to lend a hand and dedicate their lives to the sole purpose of service, even though those who are willing to help often get attacked and abused.

Someone can attack another for offering aid. We should help regardless. There is no greater feeling than seeing the smiles you have produced through giving; it is priceless. Consider the life of the man Jesus, who died on the cross for us. He led. He helped. He served. He did it all for us. He was knocked down, but it was His getting back up that matters most. He embraced His suffering, His powerlessness, His vulnerability. And He rose up.

In the end, our futures depend on how much we love, assist others in need, and think big despite receiving discouragement from others. Being raised the way I was and experiencing my accident, rehab, and my current work, I've developed a more compassionate soul, and this has given me the ability to empathize with and embrace everyone along my way. Never let your resentment tarnish your genuine self, and always rely on compassion to develop your relationships as authentically as they can be. Be sure to use your negative experiences as defining moments that help you be faithful to your purpose and accept the hard costs of remaining true to yourself.

"Be bold and courageous. When you look back on your life, you'll regret the things you didn't do more than the ones you did."

(Brown Jr. and Brown 2000)

ELEVEN

Me Against Me

One of the most disheartening dilemmas I have had since my return has been deciding whether or not I even want to be alive. I had originally told myself that I would kill myself if we lost our lawsuit against Duluth and the police, if they got away with almost killing me. Well, we lost and I'm alive, but I've questioned my purpose, why I even bothered with my life.

I would imagine that thinking of suicide is how many people react after facing a burden that seems unbearable. I would ask God why He had allowed such a thing to happen. I see now that I was feeling sorry for myself; that's all it was. I was disillusioned about my place in the world. Being here didn't seen necessary.

I wasn't recognizing that there was more to my life than suffering. The truth of the matter was, I was scared of discovering what I really was meant to do. I was scared to death. I didn't want to change my focus. I had worked diligently to get to where I was at the age of twenty, as if the world wouldn't still be there if I changed my plans. Bottom line: the world isn't going anywhere and, even though I am a few years older, I am still young.

Naturally, I was apprehensive and didn't know where to turn. So it was at this time I considered suicide. In fact, while we are discussing this unimaginable act, I must confess that this topic crosses my mind everyday. That's a pretty disturbing confession to acknowledge. Even though I know I am stronger, so much tougher than that, it is still bothersome.

We have so much to live for. When I find myself laughing at a simple memory of my favorite TV show, *Seinfeld*, I recognize that I am not being appreciative enough. What the hell am I thinking about suicide for? I don't want to die. I have a great life. I am healthy. I am strong. I have a great family and great friends. What more could I ask for?

When I wanted to learn more about service, I was introduced to an organization during the summer of 2004. That organization was Community Health Charities, which represents twenty-nine health charities in the Twin Cities dedicated to the prevention, management, and cure of chronic health conditions. These member charities raise the awareness and funds necessary to finding cures for chronic health conditions by requesting support from local businesses. Community Health Charities wrote this description about my experience:

"Nicholas re-writes the definition of perseverance. Involved in a near-fatal accident in '98, the doctors never thought he would be able to function in society again. Nicholas defied the odds and will share a story that accents the human's ability to believe in oneself and overcome any obstacle. He volunteers with the Brain Injury Association in order to communicate how support and research make the impossible possible."

How awesome is this description of the essence behind my experience? The Brain Injury Association of Minnesota was one of these twenty-nine charities. Also involved are the Alzheimer's Association, Children's Cancer Research Fund, and SAVE – Suicide Awareness Voices of Education. Learning about the last charity, SAVE, is how I was introduced to Mary.

I met Mary at a Community Health Charities training session. Mary was a very compassionate woman with an unfortunate story to tell. She had lost two children to suicide. Amy died in 1985, and Michael in 1997. Mary shared many insightful messages. She startled me by saying, "Life events don't cause suicide." So the events we experience, like losing a family member or suffering the aftermath of a TBI, do not cause suicide.

My accident then, should not lead me to such a faithless act. Yeah, I said I would do it, but it was really just an instinctive response to feeling sorry for myself. I thought that ending my life, ending my frustrations, would be an acceptable action that my supporters would be sympathetic to. My thinking was wrong. I feel terrible that I ever have such thoughts, being such an advocate for positive, motivational communication. How could I have considered doing such a thing to my family, let alone to myself?

During that first year of rehab, since I injured the side of my brain that controlled the right side of my body, my entire right half of my body was paralyzed. I was extremely weak, and lost most, if not all, functioning capability, including every fine-motor skill. This paralysis caused the right side of my face to appear droopy. This is when I really needed to continue positive self-talk. It was through venting to myself that I was able to distinguish between my negative thoughts and behaviors and my necessary actions. Generally speaking, I was being way too hard on myself and overly critical about what I could and couldn't do.

I eventually realized that, in my struggle, I was full of energy, energy to work, energy to make decisions, and energy to fuel my passion. Struggling with everything I had lost produced possibility, the possibility of living a life devoted to the service of others. I needed to come to terms with my focus, where it would fit best, and who I could help the most.

I couldn't expect everyone I knew to remain in his or her current life because I was limited. That would be a pretty selfish thing for me to expect from those I loved. With the exception of a few close friends, everyone has moved on, and that's OK. Over the last couple of years, I have really gotten to appreciate the essence behind friendship and how we, as individuals, evolve, making each relationship irreplaceable.

Paging through *O: The Oprah Magazine*, I came across an article I found extremely helpful during my acceptance stage titled, "The Good News About Bad Breaks," written by Jennifer Fields. Fields examines Paul Pearsall's book, *The Beethoven Factor*, and discusses his distinction between survivors and those who thrive because of their trauma. Pearsall disclosed his personal struggle with cancer and how he learned that, as human beings, "we thrive when suffering leads to meaning." He had found meaning after being near death and making such transitions from "languishing to flourishing" and just "surviving to savoring."

Pearsall illustrates the notion of surpassing the odds against you when he says, "Shakespeare said that we are all acting out our own dramas on the stage of life. Survivors tend to be like actors taking direction, but thrivers assume direction of their own life dramas even when the scripts contain tragedies. Thriving is defined as construing stressful events in our lives in ways that lead to new, higher levels of hardiness, happiness, healing, and hope." I didn't become fully conscious of my purpose and ability until my life was in jeopardy and my future unknown.

I realized the importance of the relationship between my mind and my body. I found myself in the worst of situations, wondering if I was strong enough to endure; I needed more than just to adapt to my TBI. I needed to thrive from it. My ordeal required a passionate state of mind, an essence that dealt with the heart and the soul.

Pearsall notes the extent to which the great composer, Beethoven, went while developing his masterpieces despite his disabling deafness. To think a man with his disabilities was able to perform at such a high level! Beethoven was unable to hear the final work he so eloquently produced. Beethoven's work will last forever; it can never be erased. Hearing his work offers me a sense of immortality, a feeling that anything is possible.

Even though my so-called "disability" will always remain, I can relate to it with great authenticity. When this topic of suicide comes up, I need to acknowledge how inauthentic, almost two-faced, I am being. Through passion, accompanied by heart, I will rejoice. I need what Pearsall terms Stress Induced Growth (SIG); this is what "thriving" is all about. I had to see the trauma and struggle I faced as stress acting as moral fiber that would restore my enduring virtues. The growth of my understanding of meaning, despite my misery, became the anchor to my prosperous journey.

So what did I find when I opened my heart? I think it is evident. If you are reading this, then you know my purpose in life: telling my story to the world, offering inspiration, offering service. I cannot play this down. I am destined to use my negative experience to help a myriad of others get past their self-doubt about who they are and to recognize that their disabilities give them the opportunity to be great.

Years ago, my friend and professor, Bill McD., developed a theory called the "Dorito Principle" that indisputably embodies my experience. A Dorito, triangular in shape, has three sides. The first side of the Dorito represents that, as human beings, we must *"seek to survive."* I think Bill might change his theory after reading Pearsall's advice to say, *"seek to thrive,"* but nevertheless, we must focus on surviving, or thriving for that matter, and yield to the unrelenting perseverance being a thriver represents. You must surrender yourself in a creative fashion. It is almost crucial to find at least one positive outcome a struggle has produced.

In my case, I found many: my resilience, my attitude, my purpose. I learned I was able to overcome an injury that my psychologist said would be the hardest thing I'd ever face. Could this be true? Definitely. I have beaten the odds and turned this horrible event into a positive life-defining moment.

The second side of the triangle represents that we must *"seek to love and be loved."* Are we capable of loving as much, if not more, after such a traumatic experience? I believe the answer is yes. After my experience unfolded, I was given a heightened level of love and compassion towards others, and my heart has never been the same. We will care more; we will offer ourselves for the sake of someone else more and always appreciate the bonds we build. My heart was forever amplified.

And finally, the most important side of the triangle tells us, *"to live for the common good."* How can I consider killing myself? It is comforting to know that I have the power to end my life; however, living for the pure gratification of what's "yet to be" embraces my passion to continue.

From telling me the Dorito Principle to teaching me about why things happen as they do, Bill gave me ideas about life and how to live. He was my professor that first summer after I began my education at St. Thomas, and the relationship that we built was profound. It's funny how the class that influenced me the most was about morality, integrity, and honesty, traits that I thought were impossible, given how my lawsuit progressed and how our attempt at establishing justice failed.

And after requesting Bill McD.'s opinion about why we undergo such extreme adversities, and receiving that article about suffering, I was left considering suffering's implications. I realized that as long we continue to have freedom, we are subject to experiencing pain, adversity, and trial. It's just life.

Eliminating false opinions others had regarding my life and seeing my life for what it was helped strengthen my faith. Furthermore, those opinions were no reason to back down. It only matters what you think of yourself and what those close to you think. Be sure to keep your head up high and your focus on the end goal, and to live for the common good. Remember, this is what really matters.

"I also want you to know my respect, my deep respect for you. Your passion for life, your passion also for academic integrity and excellence just shine in the world."

(Bill McDonough 2003)

TWELVE

Spiritual Surrender

Surrendering to the Process

O you who know my needs before I speak them
and my feelings before I express them,
thank you for the permission to grieve.
    I receive this permission as a gift in this moment.
    As I struggle to accept my loss and find healing,
    I need this gift more than any other.
Your permission to grieve reminds me
that it's okay to be lonely and sad, angry and afraid.
    Although I feel miserable right now, I can persevere,
    knowing that you don't condemn me for being human.
Free of condemnation,
I can surrender to the grief process,
learning its hard lessons on the way to rebirth.

I'm silent before you, all-wise God,
humbled by the finality of my loss,
but emboldened by your compassion
to be myself and to feel my emotions.
When I need to cry today, I will cry.
When I need to vent my anger, I will do it in a healthy way.
When I need support, I will call a friend.
And I will not be ashamed!
Where this process will lead me I do not know.
Go with me, O God, that it may lead
toward heightened awareness
and deepened character. Amen.

—*Evan Howard*

Before attending the University of St. Thomas, my relationship with God wasn't fully developed. Now, I am finally seeing the big picture. I've always believed in Him, but was far from practicing this faith. My first behavioral change came when I took a theology course with a man named Mark. This man shared his undying love for God with me during the summer of 2001. And he offered wholeheartedly a great example of the right way to have and benefit from such a relationship.

After reflecting on my past, I can't honestly say that positive things always drove me. Guilt had an obscure authority over my life and, while I was not always depressed, I was often unhappy. Beginning a relationship with Christ was unexpected; I had attended church for different reasons, mostly on Christmas and Easter. My visits were irregular. Learning about God changed my entire thought-process. I wouldn't dread going to class because my interest was now focused.

And after reflecting on the gifts I was given, I began to see God's influence. My father's Saint Christopher necklace, representing the saint of travelers, and which he gave me in 1996 when I first began my college career, sustained me. Grandpa

Jack's Bible which he took overseas slowly became part of my heart. The Saint Jude necklace Steve, a family friend, gave me offered strength, as I was not about to become a desperate case or lost cause. And from another friend, Marlys' Saint Nicholas chain protected me against the false imprisonment of my own self-defeat. How could I not think God's grace saved me?

Meeting one trial after another, I've examined myself discreetly after each failure and victory. My faith in God has been part of this from the beginning. I had to discover what was in my heart. This was a critical question I needed to ask myself when trying to understand why I was alive. Of the many cards I received while in the hospital, one from family friends Steve and Sandy, offered the following advice: *"God won't give you more than you can bear."* If this is true, I'll be able to bear anything now. I have been to hell and back, dealing with serious health issues on the way and doubt about my future and how genuine my self actually was.

Rick Warren offers so many inspiring ideas in his book, but the quotation that touches my heart the most involves how we deal with fate. Warren says, "We are products of our past, but we don't have to be prisoners of it." I needed to release myself from the hurt of my past. In time, I came to realize the extent of my parents' love and questioned the power I gave this experience.

But just after the accident I wondered how I could let something like this happen. I felt terrible. I thought about the encouragement my parents had given me to attend the University of Minnesota-Duluth; they thought it was a good place for me. Maybe I was naïve, perhaps I was scared. I should have transferred.

When I would drink in Duluth, I couldn't just have a few. The goal in Duluth was more or less about getting drunk. Some say drinking is a right of passage, but at Duluth it was more of a requirement; I see now how ridiculous it was. The football team didn't help that either. When we were freshman, we would go to the weekly parties after each home game and get trashed. So instead of being taught how to be safe under the influence, we were taught how to drink excessively. Much of that is my fault, since I always had to drink more than I could control. Then, to make matters worse, I had a difficult time seeing how troubled I was.

During my rehab, everyone could see my physical limitations; my spiritual ones, however, weren't visible. Remember 2 Corinthians 4:18? I needed to have the power of my heart and the strength of my soul unite into one. Can you achieve your dreams, especially when everything seems to be against you? Warren emphasizes the truth when he says that what we see now and today will be gone tomorrow, and those things we cannot see will last forever.

We can't predict our futures. In a split second, our lives can change for the better, or, in my case, initially for the worse, and we have little say about what the future holds. I can dream of how I'd like my life to end up, but I can't determine it. It's out of my hands, even though it seems that I am in complete control; I mean, I am the one making the decisions, choosing between yes or no, right or wrong, right?

I've often reflected on my choice to attend school in Duluth. What if I began my college career somewhere else? If that were the case, I might not have learned some pretty valuable lessons. For so long, my entire focus was on the accident itself. Maybe, however—and this is only hypothetical because who really knows for sure—I might not have learned the value of commitment as well as I have, or the value of friendship and family, the cost of living, the worth of exercise, the value of community, my passion, or God's purpose for my life. I may not have learned how a smile can brighten someone's day, the importance of love, going that extra mile, and finally, the value of personal relationships.

For every single bad thing that happens to you there are multiple benefits. Remember, it can't rain all the time, and the sun will shine once again. View every situation positively; it might be a critical turning point in your life. Since I had never been encouraged to give up, the thought of surrendering myself didn't seem the way to face something positively.

If you look at it from a spiritual perspective, you can see that surrendering sometimes to these difficult times and events is exactly what we need to do. They are like a kick in the ass, helping us to get back on track. So many people fall victim to their problems and feel lost, trapped. But maybe if they saw the situation from a different perspective, they might climb themselves out more easily.

When I was at the bottom, discouraged and angry, the only place to go was up. Here, my attitude was my greatest asset. Remember occupational therapy? After fighting it, I began to see everything I could gain, and you know what? My therapists, Elin and Sue, kept saying I was on my way, on my way back into the light, I was climbing out of hell. I was making strides. In some respect, I surrendered myself to OT, to the efforts of two wonderful people who saw more in me than I saw in myself. They were true saviors, angels in disguise.

Why continue denying God's presence when there is so much in your heart that says otherwise? How can something so hidden be so powerful? We can't see Him, and we can't see His presence. Or can we? Miracles occur everyday. To see them you just have to open your heart and lower your guard.

More often than not, we miss seeing miracles because of self-will and stubbornness, and we question God's presence. Our mindsets have to change if we are ready to witness miracles everyday. We are required to look with soft eyes, and see the miracles found in weakness. Remember, God loves using weakness to embody strengths.

As I continued my rehab at Sister Kenny, my heart was calling out for me to take advantage of the situation. Giving up was never really an option. It was when I started to talk again that I began to remember more things. I remember seeing all the patients on the unit, and making myself a promise that I would never give less than 110 percent until I was satisfied with where I was. It's funny; I never really became satisfied, so giving my progress everything I have plus some has never stopped.

Warren says that, "your commitments can develop you or they can destroy you, but either way, they will define you." I was committed to using this struggle as a stepping-stone for developing my life. Remember those defining moments and how we can choose to define them or they will define us? It's quite simple, actually. Warren highlights the idea that life is supposed to be difficult, and it is through these difficult times that we grow the most. This experience has helped me grow physically, emotionally, and most of all, spiritually, through developing positive personal relationships with others and myself.

I was sent a card by one of my Bulldog teammates, Tom, as I was enduring rehab that said, "The Lord didn't promise that LIFE would be easy, but He did PROMISE to go with you every step of the way." This card represented the glory that was possible if I changed my self-defeating attitude. Maybe this whole experience was meant to fortify my character. Warren suggests, "Every problem is a character building opportunity, and the more difficult it is, the greater the potential for building spiritual muscle and moral fiber." Yes, the quotation from the film *Big Fish* is applicable to many places in our lives.

Remember that famous quotation by Franklin Roosevelt about the essence of glory. He said, "Pain is temporary, glory lasts forever." He said this after the Pearl Harbor massacre. It's true. Glory will always be remembered; it is, after all, immortal. Yes, the burden may be heavy, and you may feel inclined to quit. It's probably heavier than anything you've ever had to carry. But keep in mind the strength of your heart and what you will yield in the end.

This attitude provides the makings of a champion, someone who is beaten down, left behind, but who then defines what is possible. Nobody said you were going to glide through life on a flat plane. However, if you maintain the proper faith fueled by enough passion, you would never be disappointed, and that's a fact.

Another favorite quotation of mine by Warren says, "You owe it to future generations to preserve the testimony of how God helped you fulfill his purposes on earth." That's it. That's my purpose. I need to use this entire ordeal, one that should have crippled me and left me broken, as my motivation to change the world one inch at a time.

My friend, Matt, whom I've known since high school, told me that I had, "labored the past two years, built character, a tough skin, and an idea about success and what it entails. It is life experience, not education, that truly shapes and molds an individual." Hearing Matt's encouraging words was crucial in my progress. I had thought that I was weak and worthless. Matt's words motivated me to focus on the path I was on knowing that it could benefit me. What I lost wasn't important; it didn't matter. One event will not make or break you, even though many of us fall victim to thinking so.

After seeing Don, a family friend, recover from an abdominal aortic aneurysm and continue his life, defying the odds of just becoming a memory, I realized that being tough is not a myth or generalization. Examples from our older generation, such as Don's, show that actual people can take on and fulfill difficult challenges, proving it is a person's experience that influences the toughness of his or her character.

Do not a let a single moment of failure define you. It takes more than one event to bring a person to his or her knees and to bring me down to mine. Be faithful; trust in the power of faith, and in the power behind the possibilities your difficulties carry. My accident, this faith-building episode, not only deepened my convictions, but helped me to identify feelings of guilt and resentment, and to see the true potential this experience offered.

Remember, life is made up of a series of experiences that mold and shape who you are. And in most cases, since we are our own worst enemy, we constantly criticize ourselves through a lack of confidence that is fueled by our own stubbornness. I gave up the story that I was a victim and chose faithfully to see this struggle through to the end.

One should not have to go through life feeling sorry for oneself, kicking one's own ass, and making life unbearable. This race, whether it entails a severe loss or a tragic moment, always ends up being a race against yourself, right? You are your own worst enemy. Do not let your own fear influence what's going to happen in the end. It will only lead you into misery and despair. This much I promise. So please, keep the faith.

"If this is the right thing to do, I will do it no matter what goes against me, or how tough things become. I will never weaken and I will never give up. 'For God hath not given me the spirit of fear; but of power, and of love, and of a sound mind.'"

(Peale 1994)

4:44 ● AM

THIRTEEN

Moment in Time

I feel obligated to stress the uncertainty others had regarding my homecoming. Supposedly, it was impossible. I was hurt too badly; my injuries were too severe. I might as well have been shipped off to a nursing home where I'd forever remain without this purpose. I was never coming back. I really can't imagine what everyone experienced those first few weeks in Duluth. I hear stories, but I will never grasp the severity of that time in Duluth. From my parents, my sister, my grandparents, to my aunts and uncles, my best friends, my coaches, and everyone else there, I get ideas of what it was like, but I can not really know for myself.

Throughout this chapter, I will acknowledge some of the defining moments during my time in the hospital, but realize that I am drawing solely on the knowledge, insights, stories, and recollections others have told me. This tells what those close to me experienced in Duluth, and how they endured.

After the phone call arrived in Bloomington that Sunday morning, the shocking vision of their forsaken son compelled my family to start a journey through the depths of hell, with its confrontation with the Duluth Police Department. My parents were told that I was in the Intensive Care Unit and that they had better hurry, for my life might end at any moment.

And after being told that I had fled a vehicle and ended up taking a thirty-five-foot plunge into Chester Creek where I almost drowned, they were told they should be prepared to deal with charges being pressed against me. My parents knew that they had raised me well enough and that I wouldn't jeopardize the life of others, or my own for that matter, by driving while intoxicated.

Did my parents ever question that maybe what they taught me didn't set in? Did they question my ability to know right from wrong? After all, so many people get behind the wheel after spending hours at the bar and actually think they have the mental capacity to operate a massive killing machine. What my parents were about to find out went far beyond their wildest imaginings.

I would never drive under the influence. My sister kept saying, "*Nick would never drive drunk. He just wouldn't. He's told me time and time again to never, ever drive drunk. He just would never do that.*" There must be some sort of mix-up. But a hospital chaplain, of all people, a man of God, had talked with them and he couldn't have lied.

Fact: I was at the scheduled party, which began on Saturday night after dinner. I would imagine Andy drove to the party and we started to drink. As I've said, I don't remember that day and I can't say for certain what exactly happened. We know that the party was busted, that many drinkers were underage. One of the officers "busting" the party said I attempted to hide upstairs since I didn't want to receive yet another minor consumption ticket. One report said I was found underneath a bed, and was escorted downstairs.

Another fact: it's impossible to escape a surrounded party house, especially when you're trashed. I was caught and apparently got in line to get my ticket. Apparently someone said I was talking to Allison, a friend, outside the house afterwards and began walking home. The article in the newspaper said I had snuck out. Funny how our investigation documented the time of my friend Allison's citation at 2:13 am, and I was seen talking to Allison outside, on the sidewalk; if I had snuck out and hadn't received a ticket, I wouldn't have been seen talking to Allison.

I have a hard time discerning between what really happened and the mindless chaos I find when I try to retrieve anything of that previous week in Duluth. At the scene of the fall, I was labeled a "*Code Green*" by the Gold Cross rescuers, which was, as I later found out, critical. This code alerted the staff at St. Luke's that they were about to receive a victim with a "life-threatening multi-trauma." Life threatening? Multi-trauma? I wasn't declared dead at any point; however, my heart did stop on the creek bed. CPR was required; my life was in grave danger. It's hard to comprehend this level of distress, and I sometimes think it was only a nightmare.

The rescue team took me out of the creek, after I had been *anointed* by the dirty, filthy, polluted water; I was unresponsive and practically dead. I showed no spontaneous movement. My meeting with God was under way. The near drowning posed the biggest threat. My capacity to take in oxygen was gone. My life was in jeopardy; my future, unknown. The prophecy was right; the journey back would be long and grueling.

The ambulance brought me to St. Luke's at 3:35 a.m. The delivery of my lifeless body to St. Luke's was far from pretty. Upon my arrival, the admitting physician took charge and did what was necessary to keep my body alive. My pulse and respirations were above average, and erratic. The amount of oxygen I was getting was 78 percent, far below the required 90 percent. My blood pressure was 83/40. The normal range is somewhere between 90-140/80-60. Obviously, my body wanted to call it quits; my soul, however, saw differently.

As I was taken into the ICU, it's as if the world stopped. At any moment, I could have died. For the sake of my mental stability, I was lucky to not have been awake for this. My body was there; my mind was somewhere else. Perhaps God was giving me direction, as the journey ahead would prove defining. I am certain He was there. If this were not true, my strength would not have spoken for itself.

And, when my father saw my body in the ICU, lacking signs of life, a sense of calmness filled his mind. When he asked God to save his son, just as God saved Christ Jesus, my future was placed under His verdict. My hospital room was filled with supporters; everyone came. Family came from all over. I do wish I had been conscious for this; apparently, it was about uniting, engaging, and receiving. Luckily, I was able to re-live some hilarious moments and get a secondhand image of how the days passed.

The ambiguity of my condition increased by the hour. The doctors had said that death was near and it was impossible for me to recover from such an injury. My body was severely traumatized. Every indication of life is a hopeful sign when such a high level of uncertainty exists. From a slight squeeze to the blink of an eye, small gestures offered hope that I was still there inside a broken body. I was in a coma for six weeks. And the simple gestures, such as a firm squeeze from my left hand didn't go unnoticed.

My mom wrote, "It truly was a miracle that you were still with us. You were coming around little by little. One day I was talking to you like I had been for days, I just knew you could hear me, I called you 'Naughty Nick' and you grabbed my hand on the right and Dad's hand on the left. It was wonderful, our first sign that you were there." There were so many signs implying my readiness to embark on this journey.

My mom describes how my friends really took a stand to help bring me back. She wrote, "You really respond to your friends and it is wonderful to see. I really cannot describe the way your friends have been here for you. They all really truly love you and it is plain to see. You are so lucky to have all these special friends in your life. Kim and Sean come up almost every day. Kim can really get you going. Apparently you gave her the finger and bit her last night. What a great response, huh!"

Hearing everyone's personal insight about the time in Duluth and at Sister Kenny contributes to my knowledge and appreciation of those who were there. One of the more meaningful stories I was told about my stay at St. Luke's involves the insights and attitudes of one of my primary nurses. His ability to help my parents cope with what they were about to endure was amazing.

When my family was feeling the impact of my severe list of injuries, the nursing staff was there, offering support and insight about the reality of my future. One nurse in particular at St. Luke's, Art, told my parents that it was going to be a long road, but if I could be as strong as everyone said I was, it would soon be just a bad dream. It would take time, he said, but they had to be patient. Do not rush.

Art was another angel on my shoulders. My parents were comforted by his words of hope. I mean, he had probably seen it all, and my situation was no different. The outcome was indisputably given by the grace of God, and was similar to miracles Art had seen before.

My father, when we were discussing Duluth, said that perhaps Art was an angel sent down from heaven, and as quickly as he arrived to save me, he would vanish once I was transferred to Minneapolis. God's strength is unlimited and can never be matched. Was Art one of God's messengers? He was there to help me heal, and to give my parents the reassurance they needed. They were about to lose me forever, and there was nobody else to bring me back except the one person who had seen everything. The Lord's grace gave me strength.

Once I became conscious, I couldn't understand this. I felt like I was the only one losing, the only one in pain. I was out of joint with reality and didn't witness the pain of others. Paul Pearsall, author of *The Beethoven Factor*, writes, "No matter how personally we feel the sting of adversity in our lives, crises happen to systems, not individuals. As hurt as we feel, we never hurt alone." I wasn't witnessing their struggle and how my own was bringing me closer to God. This was difficult for me; I felt it was my fault they were unhappy. I then of course felt the extreme guilt associated with causing this unwarranted pressure in the lives of those I loved. I was ignorant.

At this moment, God commandeered; He took over. Luke 18:27 says, *"all things are possible."* Never turn your back on the possibilities of tomorrow. Never tell yourself that something is impossible, because as you will discover, one more attitude change might be all it takes. So many people rant and rave about their inability to accomplish impossible feats or about the lack of skill they may have. This is garbage; absolute nonsense. Never let some random beholder tell you what you can or can't do. If it is in your heart, you will find a way.

It's never just ability but also the resilience of your heart that will lead you to achieving your dreams. Eleanor Roosevelt supported this idea, saying, "Believe in yourself. You gain strength, courage, and confidence by every experience in which you stop to look fear in the face. You must do that which you think you cannot do."

Take Roosevelt's words to heart as you seek to accomplish your goals. Maintain a positive outlook on your own life; never forget to always look fear straight in the eyes. Not fully supporting my life and not believing in myself led to my thinking that I would automatically fail before I even began. It took me a long time to get my confidence up to a working level and some things are still difficult. In fact, they will always be hard. Some things were hard before I was injured; they won't magically get any easier after this.

Nevertheless, I have found a way to be satisfied with what I have, which has allowed things to happen more easily. It is weird how that happens, how the harder you try, the more difficult something becomes. But when you take a step back and let things develop naturally, they become easy; they become yours. You had actually made it harder than you ought to. Perhaps that is maturity, or education. Remember, challenges are never life or death, so don't give away your power to a lack of belief. One of my favorite movies, *Tin Cup*, about the struggles of an infamous golfer, offers a most inspiring review. "In love and sports, playing it safe can't hold a candle to taking risks and acting from the heart."

There are so many inspiring, hopeful messages out there; we just need to keep our eyes and ears open. You never know how the next movie, next song, next book, or next experience is going to move you. Just keep yourself available without being too stubborn to try new things. It's just like surrendering, isn't it?

Try comparing the Titanic to the Arc from the Old Testament. Remember how professionals developed the Titanic, using the greatest technology by the best engineers. We all know it as the boat that was never supposed to sink, but did just that. The Arc, on the other hand was built by amateurs without the up-to-date technology and a slew of trained engineers, and this boat bore its passengers safely to the dry land.

It's so inspiring when we see or hear stories, successes, or simple quotations that show the strength and relentless drive of the human spirit. So please remember that Rome wasn't built in a day; it was built brick by brick, and you will become stronger by living through adversity. Nobody said life was going to be easy and that is probably the biggest self-evident truth we must accept.

There is something heroic in dealing positively with struggle. It offers hope, courage, and an idea about living purposefully. This is where I began focusing when I realized I was in a situation that only offered two choices. I could either be held hostage to myself, which would surely lead to my demise, or give sacrificially and champion myself without an ounce of fear. You can never look back. I have always been a worrier, worrying about everything, or maybe, given the extenuating circumstances, I should say warrior. Warrior is more fitting. When it came down to getting my life back, this became obvious.

Persevering through an intense hospital experience is difficult, even nearly impossible, without getting personal, heartfelt, emotional reassurance. So many factors surface once one realizes how overwhelming it can be. It is especially difficult if you enter the hospital unconscious, where you are entirely in the hands of those looking out for your health and safety.

I went into this battle blindfolded. I was at the mercy of people I'd never met. As I had mentioned before, I was near death. It was a miracle that I even made it through that first night. I can't picture myself in such terrible shape as I sit here writing my thoughts without any first hand knowledge of how it truly was.

I have pictures, but I have a hard time feeling the boy in the picture is me; it can't be me. So many machines were keeping me alive. It is still difficult to face the truth, even when I take my shirt off and see the discolored tracheotomy scar in the middle of my throat. It's just a little unbelievable. However, as I imagine myself lying there comatose, I experience a feeling that truly expresses my having been on a fearless crusade.

It felt like I was dreaming when I actually realized that I had been relying on a respirator, that I was injured so badly and needed a machine to help me breathe. My mom's journal of that experience helped me grasp how serious it was. She wrote, "On Sunday, October 11th at 6 a.m. they took you off the respirator and let you go. You never needed it again. Another miracle."

I often recall the movie *Any Given Sunday* in which a character gives a pre-game motivational speech that describes going into a battle without fear. This speech, given by Al Pacino's character, the head coach, is one of the most stimulating scenes I have ever seen. I guarantee you will be inspired and motivated, even if you don't play football. Pacino's words can be applied to your life and every difficulty you face.

Pacino's character, Tony D'Amato, expresses encouragement to his team by saying, "You find out life's this game of inches, so is football. Because in either game—life or football—the margin for error is so small. I mean, one half a step too late or too early and you don't quite make it. One half second too slow, too fast and you don't quite catch it. The inches we need are everywhere around us. They're in every break of the game, every minute, every second. On this team we fight for that inch. On this team we tear ourselves and everyone else around us to pieces for that inch."

Pacino's character also emphasizes his passion by saying, "I'll tell you this, in any fight it's the guy who's willing to die who's gonna win that inch. And I know, if I'm gonna have any life any more it's because I'm still willing to fight and die for that inch, because that's what living is, the six inches in front of your face. Now I can't make you do it. You've got to look at the guy next to you, look into his eyes. Now I think you're going to see a guy who will go that inch with you. You're gonna see a guy who will sacrifice himself for this team, because he knows when it comes down to it you're gonna do the same for him."

If you apply the same standards Pacino's character emphasizes to your life, you won't be left wondering, wondering if you had done everything, wondering if you've worked hard enough, wondering if…yeah. You won't be left wondering. That's all I am saying. You do not want to be left questioning yourself by the lack of effort you may or may not have applied, and in the end, you will know you had given it everything.

I want to emphasize the most poignant phrase from the speech. This is the part I feel is especially meaningful and I think it applies to most struggles in the same way it applies to mine.

The most meaningful reference is about the importance of each *inch*. We all know that our lives can change in the blink of an eye, the equivalent to this infamous inch. It's so small, so short. But an inch is all it takes for something to impact our life. In a matter of seconds or the distance of an inch, our lives can change, for better or worse. Yes, I almost died, I lost all my skills, I was hurting.

But if you consider the extent of my injuries and the initial diagnosis, I can't honestly say that I didn't win. Maybe I did not win in court, where a couple of judges had to deal with a severely distorted view of reality. But where it really mattered, in life, in God's eyes, I have won tremendously. I won my life back. I won a new perspective.

So many people aren't willing to see all the good something bad has brought them. At first, I was like this; I was stubborn. I hated how my life was going. I didn't believe in my parents, my family, my friends, or myself. I had been let down; I was disappointed. I had a bad attitude.

As human beings, when tragedy strikes, we often focus on every wrong choice we have made. Whenever I reflect on my past, I still feel a great deal of anxiety because I know I shouldn't have been so intent on earning the respect of my teammates by drinking. Nothing I did was ever enough. But I know that focusing on this doesn't help me move forward.

The events that happened in Duluth were simply educational and they occurred during a time in my life when I wish I had made better choices. That is what it came down to, choices, making the choice to champion myself, accepting this experience for what it was worth rather than living in denial. My strength here, once again, speaks for itself.

Life is, and never will be, fair. The truth remains that when I first regained consciousness maybe I didn't give myself enough credit and feel enough gratitude for all that I did have. I struggled with this. I didn't recognize my ability to overcome such a disaster. I've finally moved beyond looking for excuses.

Early in my rehab, when I took a good look in the mirror and saw the man staring back at me, I didn't like who I saw. I wasn't confident. This was my brain injury speaking. I questioned myself more than I should have, while making the word "can't" a common part of my vocabulary simply because of all my weaknesses at the time. I thought: I am a failure; I am weak; I am not enough.

Losing was probable. Most things worth achieving are hardly reached on the first attempt anyway. This is where your heart comes in, where your commitment finally pays off, and you are there, victorious. Many people fail because they quit too soon; they don't give it a fair effort. They lose the moment they said it was impossible, and this attitude, well, it sure as hell wasn't good for a young man trying to reclaim his life.

When we work towards something, the outcome will most likely be decided by a small margin, inch by inch. In other words, the outcome could go either way, but it is the small details that make a world of difference. Something as simple as fine-tuning a skill every single day, for example, might mean the difference between being promoted or remaining stuck in that dead-end job.

Taking that extra step to show you are committed might be the turning point in deciding your fate. Be courageous as you find yourself against all odds, when there are only two minutes left. This is the time you need to make a decision. Will you remain where you are, or will you start moving towards where you ought to be? It is as simple as that, making that choice.

Have you ever heard the phrase "*The look in your eyes tells everything?*" Well, it is true. We can see so many strong characteristics in a person's eyes: courage, heart, desire, fear, resentment. I am not sure what everyone saw in my eyes when I was unconscious, lying there near death.

But I can tell you what they didn't see. They didn't see defeat. They didn't see a quitter, or someone who would walk away without a fight. Once my confidence improved, and once I had made a few decisive strides, this look in my eyes became even stronger. I was done feeling sorry for myself.

Any time you are faced with the seriousness of existence, you are best realizing that this will be a long, challenging road.

I faced my toughest battle—against myself. I could not give in to the fear of my own self-doubt before sacrificing myself to the greater good of the world and the impending success I was so close to achieving. It came down to how badly I truly wanted it, and how much heart I, in fact, truly had.

"The credit belongs to those people who are actually in the arena, who know the great enthusiasms, the great devotions to a worthy cause. Who at best, know the triumph of high achievement; and who, at worst, fail while daring greatly…so that their place shall never be with those cold and timid souls who know neither victory nor defeat."

(Theodore Roosevelt)

FOURTEEN

Moving Forward

Keeping Your Perspective

The child in me expects life to be fair, O God.
It seems only right that good people
Should be protected from tragedy,
that only bad people should suffer.
    But often the opposite happens.
    The wrong people prosper,
    and the wrong people get hurt.
When victimized by unfairness,
I throw inner tantrums of rage.
I lose my center in your love and see life not as
a gift from your hand but as a chamber of horrors.
    I need a new perspective,
    a more mature way of looking at things.
    Once I stop expecting fairness,

I can appreciate life for what it is,
not for what I wish it were.
When realism tempers my naivete,
I make wiser choices and become
Less vulnerable to disappointment.
> *Put to death the childishness within me, O Lord.*
> *Help me to accept life on its own terms,*
> *realizing that its potential for suffering*
> *enriches its joys.*
When tragedy strikes, remind me that
you still have the last word.
Increase my resiliency in the face of unfairness.
As you care for the birds of the air
and the flowers of the field,
so do I ask you to care for me. Amen.

—*Evan Howard*

Appreciating what I received from the people at Sister Kenny wasn't ever difficult. But before I truly recognized what they were doing for me, weeks and months had passed; I had made progress such as graduating from a hospital bed to a wheelchair, from a wheelchair to walking, from lifting two pounds to lifting ten.

I can't even recall being only able to lift only two pounds. It's almost embarrassing. I am the type of person who doesn't enjoy waiting for something to happen. I like things to happen immediately. And being able to only lift two pounds posed a challenge, a significant one.

The people I met at Sister Kenny were extraordinary. When I first arrived there in 1998, my case had been assigned to a certain social worker who thought the answer to our prayers was to let me waste away in a nursing home. What a poor excuse for someone whose job was to assist families during times of crisis. I can't stress it enough how ridiculous this person's view sounds when I hear the story, from my parent's perspective, of that day she made this recommendation.

Perhaps my parents were so distraught that they misinterpreted her intentions. I don't know, but she didn't have the right attitude. My mom broke down. My dad got upset. At that moment, my nurse, Kristi, and my occupational therapist, Lynette, spoke up on my behalf. They had seen signs, or at least a sliver of hope, behind all the fear.

Someone suggested that maybe the social worker thought that a nursing home might be a starting point, and that since the stress level was so high, my parents took the suggestion the wrong way. I saw this social worker when I was making my comeback, before I knew of her initial recommendation, and she avoided eye contact. So I am just guessing that she knew she made a terrible mistake.

Don't you hate it when other people don't believe in you? Besides that one exception, my experience at Sister Kenny was a special one. I had great nurses, great therapists, and great doctors. And I met some great patients who were walking paths similar to mine. We were all working to get our lives back. After reflecting on my Sister Kenny experience, I've realized a couple important reminders.

It is apparent that everyone has his or her own individual cross to bear. Some have fairly large crosses, while others have smaller ones. Regardless of the size, everyone has, or will eventually have, something difficult to bear. That's just life. We can try and try to prevent this, but sometimes bad things happen, often without our consent.

My most challenging event that I remember—and I don't know how I should interpret it and I wish it had never happened—happened late one night when I was in bed. This bed was designed to keep me protected; it was like a huge cage, with a mesh barrier to keep me from getting out and falling.

I hadn't had a bowel movement for some time and the nurse was concerned. If I was at all aware, I would have been concerned too. So I was given a suppository before bed. Those usually aren't comfortable to receive. And picture this: I woke up during the middle of the night and, to my surprise, found that the suppository had worked; I had a BM. I pushed the call light requesting assistance. But as my bad luck for the night continued, nobody came.

I hit the call light again and again; nobody came. At this point, I became agitated. Remember that my mental capacity was somewhere between that of an infant or toddler at this point; I am surprised I even remember this. I took my pants off and began to smear the remains of my BM on the walls of my bed. If I had had any bit of common sense at the time, I would never have done that. I mean, it was disgusting. Nobody in his or her right mind would ever make a mess out of his or her feces. But I remember doing just that.

Remembering myself lying in my own excrement, I finally understand the truth behind humility. Just knowing this event was part of my past is reason enough for me to empathize with anyone, anytime, anywhere. However, I am sad to say that I didn't appreciate this lesson until years after the actual event. Sometimes we don't understand the message until long after the so-called defining moment has passed. We reflect on that one thing without comprehension. We usually focus on the negative right away. And when we are so focused on the bad, we forget about all the good.

Hearing another's experience offers companionship. It is much easier to battle a disease or an injury when you can join hands with others who share the same difficulty. Women with breast cancer unite to raise money to contribute to a cure. And I know that, one day, women won't have to worry anymore. It is sad to know that some young people become sick or injured and must spend the rest of their lives in nursing homes without the companionship of other recovering thrivers. Having to rely on someone else feeding you is really a difficult task to accept. I have fed many people at the hospital, and it's very humbling to help with such a routine task.

And what about diapers? Let's call them what they are. Having to wear them is just another thing that requires someone to swallow his or her pride and realize that it is OK to ask for help. So many people out there are more than willing to lend a helping hand. Having to wear diapers or to help someone who wears them means recognizing vulnerability. Many don't understand the feeling of vulnerability. Perhaps these individuals aren't called to God's work.

People get multiple sclerosis or polio. People become quadriplegics. Cancer strikes. There are so many things that can appear out of nowhere. I had very little firsthand knowledge of such things and I never really understood their impact. Recognizing that these aren't punishments, even though they may seem to be, is necessary. It isn't God hurting us, and they are not caused by anything we have done. It is simply life, a life that just so happened to take a turn for the worse. The problem with our society is that we are so quick to blame others and not recognize our roles and what we can do.

Like I said, I wanted nothing more than to make the city of Duluth accountable for its part in my pain. I was overlooking the big picture; I wanted revenge. I wanted Matthew 7:15 to pay for the fall, for the lies, and for the accident. It only seemed fair that he and the city be held accountable. But as I have already said, life is not fair, and good people get hurt. I had never realized how many good people get abused every day.

There's no disputing that life is extremely hard; it's painful. People get hurt. People die. It is hard to find the good amidst so much bad. I think if you look closely though, you normally find it where you'd least expect it. I found a more passionate level of self-actualization after many days of resentment and fear had passed. As it turned out, this new focus has led me to become more and more of what I am supposed to be. The Army's recruiting axiom describes this quest perfectly:

"Be all that you can be."

Surely this will mean different things to different people, but the concept is generally universal. Living up to our potentials is the only thing we should ever expect from ourselves. So many people give in to the pressures they experience and the struggles they endure. Enduring was necessary for me to develop into what I was supposed to become. Yes, it was painful. My strength and endurance was tested. I was, of course, unsure if I could handle it, that the pain might be too much. My weakness was in the arms of the one thing I never imagined possible.

But remember, God often uses weakness as a means to an end. My weakness let others know that the pain was in fact real; but after I adopted a more proactive approach, I saw the struggle to the very end. It never got the best of me, and I showed everyone that I would never back down. I would survive; I would, in fact, thrive. I tackled this traumatic brain injury with everything I had. It required a strategic, yet open, game plan that was developed by my soul. I would be all that I was capable of becoming, and then some.

The true glory isn't left for those who go into a battle half-heartedly; it is for those whose courage knows no boundaries. There was nothing preventing me from this glory except my own inner conflict against myself. My therapists at Sister Kenny taught me that the choice was mine. I could either choose to apply myself with conviction, or I could remain where I was and ultimately fail. And I never favored losing, which is what I saw would happen if I didn't make the right choice.

I figured that if I can inspire others just like those who inspired me, I would make a worthwhile conclusion to an accident that should have left me a heartbreaking memory. There is so much to relay; I only hope I am articulating it as perfectly as those who came before me did. Most people never get to experience this level of humility, and if they do, they either blow it off completely or find themselves in perpetual failure.

I needed to accept help from others, particularly those at Sister Kenny, but also indirectly from my friends and family, while knowing that it didn't signify weakness, but rather, courage. As I mentioned previously, I wrestled with the idea of actually needing occupational therapy, because I couldn't see the benefits. I didn't want to accept the help Sue and Elin were offering me. I recall them asking me to organize documents into appropriate folders, and only giving it a half-assed effort. I did not see the benefit.

I was desperate, especially after being visited by friends and seeing how well they were doing. I saw no reason to learn organization skills. I didn't see my purpose. It was difficult for me to see everyone so much further ahead in life than I was. It was at this time in my life that I thought I'd better find a more suitable idea of who I was before I gave up, which would be an utterly pointless moment of desperation. It was at this moment I saw the man I mentioned previously, Dave Pelzer on Oprah Winfrey's afternoon television show.

I received his book, *Help Yourself,* for Christmas and with his permission, I have included some of his chapter reminders, which are, by far, some of the most meaningful, genuine, pieces of writing I have ever read. I'd like to share his insights with you now, as they have had the most profound impact on my life.

This book not only changed my attitude but it is probably the reason I am still alive today. His story makes my experience look pathetic in comparison. I am amazed by his endurance, his ability, and his perseverance to overcome a seemingly impossible situation. He is a remarkable person, and I owe him more than he could possibly imagine.

But really, based on his own struggle, I am sure he understands. So, without further ado, Pelzer's gift awaits you. I hope you are able to see his genius as much as I do. Nothing compares to his inspiring and self-fulfilling reminders. The ones that were more meaningful to my journey are in bold and enlarged. However, they are all poignant and encouraging. I didn't include every one, just my favorites. Buy his book; you won't be disappointed. This much I promise.

Dave Pelzer's
Help Yourself Reminders

☒ **Let go of a past you cannot change.**

☒ If you feel guilty about what has transpired, make amends as best as you can, and if possible turn it around and use it as a stepping-stone to make things happen.

☒ Above all, it's your life and your choice.

☒ **Forgiveness allows you to be cleansed and helps to ease your pain.**

☒ **Defining moments or situations can be a positive catalyst as the turning point in your life.**

☒ **Before you quit on yourself when life isn't fair, exhaust all your options for making things happen.**

☒ No one takes anything away from us, unless we give up on ourselves first.

☒ A consistent, positive attitude makes a world of difference.

☒ Your day starts with what you say to yourself.

☒ Focus, Focus, Focus: Where are you at in your life? What are you doing to make things better? And where are you going?

☒ **A little bit of adversity can help to re-align you, make you humble, and make you want it more.**

And, as I read his book, I took note of the more meaningful statements, which weren't included in the chapter reminders.

☒ Step up to the plate.

☒ If you don't believe in yourself, how can you gain the trust and respect of others?

☒ That for everything in life we desire, we have to be willing to forfeit something for our cause.

☒ The only element stopping you is you.

Taking to heart Pelzer's reminders seriously will change your life. Believe me: you will begin to see your life through new eyes. I know I did.

"Nothing can dominate the hunger, the unstoppable drive, of the human spirit. Nothing. Just don't quit on yourself."

(Pelzer 2000)

FIFTEEN

Knowledge Through Experience

Attending college in Duluth didn't develop me fully, even though I did well academically. I was more interested in meeting new people and socializing. But it wasn't until I was taken out of that environment that I saw the true benefits of education. Being a UMD Bulldog turned out to be a better learning experience than attending any of the classes I took there.

Coach Moe and Coach Vinny were the two people who contributed most to my character. Coach Moe was influential because he was still doing what he loved, coaching football, even at his age. From what I hear of the early days of my stay at St. Luke's, when I was critical and near death, I know he was a definite life-support for many of the brokenhearted. My father expressed his gratitude to the coach's visits by telling me about Coach's attitude.

Whenever I showed signs of improvement, Coach would offer some football analogy, saying something like "Nick made another first down," or "He's getting close to the end zone." By using sports analogies, he turned the situation into something of a game, while showing how it truly came down to a matter of inches. I would either win or lose based on how I played, how I fought for every inch. Did I possess the ingenuity, let alone the muscle, to overcome such a trauma? The answer to this question surely unfolded as the days passed and the months went by.

People like my coach saw my physical disabilities; my heart and spirit were less evident. Showing these was left for me and me alone. It's one thing to blow out a knee and undergo rehab to regain mobility. But it is another thing to experience severe head trauma and fight your way back. At this point, there was no assurance I would ever be the same again. I like to think I can do more now. I have more knowledge, more passion, and a stronger purpose. Plus, now I know I can accomplish anything. I've gained the confidence because of people like Coach Moe.

Observing the way he coached on the field furnished me with ideas about commitment, loyalty, and the way our personal obligation contributes to our immortality. Coach showed me the true nature behind being a living success, that it is more than simply having a job or career; it is a way of life.

I was told that Coach chastised the police about how underage drinking had been going on for years, and that the way they had acted was a disgrace. He was disappointed in Duluth, a city in which he was so renowned, so respected. How could something like this happen? Coach's attitude helped many to see that I would be OK; he might have even been one of those angels I spoke of earlier. He visited me daily, stopping by for just a few moments to offer strength.

Coach Vinny taught me about being a genuinely good person. He was also up at the hospital a lot during those early, horrible days. I don't think Matthew 7:15 had any idea about what he had caused. If he could have seen the pain we were all in, he might have sought forgiveness. But he never did. Integrity is such a hard trait to come by these days, so I'm not surprised that he failed to show it.

Coach Vinny cared deeply about his job as head coach and he cared more about his players than he did about himself. Vinny has proven to be a comfort to my friends and family. So many of God's messengers were with me.

I felt like I let him down for not being responsible enough to get home safely. Getting through the guilt that accompanied this was tough. I don't remember that week, so I don't remember Coach Vinny's speech to us players about underage drinking. Apparently he felt terrible about his speech to us that week and my subsequently avoiding the police. And when Coach Vinny visited me at Abbott, I balled my eyes out. Even though I was semi-comatose, I knew deep down inside I had failed him.

But the reality of what occurred is a mystery. I don't think I escaped the barricaded house without receiving a ticket that night, so I don't think I tried to run away. In all honesty, I think I was just too drunk to think straight. When I was walking home I probably thought I would get another ticket, so I tried my best to avoid Matthew 7:15. And as a result, one thing led to another, and I fell. As I've said, I don't remember a dog, and I don't remember hiding behind a garbage bin. All I know is that I was made out to be a delinquent, and seven years later, I am trying to describe this event, and my life after it, as best I can.

In the spring of 2000, I attended Normandale Community College, where I took two classes, just to get back into the college atmosphere. I had originally wanted to start at the University of Minnesota, but after a campus tour, I realized I would have more problems there due to its massive size. My parents kept suggesting a smaller university, but of course, I was stubborn again. I envisioned having such a great time being a Minnesota Gopher, but I wasn't looking at all the angles.

As fate had it, I finished my college career at the University of St. Thomas in St. Paul, Minnesota. This was an experience of a lifetime. I met so many incredible people who contributed to my life, and I can't imagine not knowing them. Was this part of His plan? I know I was meant to be there. It was more than just a school for me. Everything I learned, the people I met, and the confidence I gained by going there is a huge part of my knowing and living out my purpose.

Negative feelings have almost destroyed me, and I've witnessed people struggle for existence in our cynical world. I've thought: no wonder people turn to drugs, alcohol, and violence. These help mask the pain. Life's not fair. And it's not easy. But struggle does offer you an opportunity to appreciate your life, regardless of all the hardship you endure.

While studying in my major, the discipline of communication studies, I met a few people who offered me endless opportunity. Dr. Bernard Armada and Dr. Tom Endres taught me not only about the field of communication, but about life itself. And Kim Schumann, my advisor and director of disability services, gave me the support I needed to further my learning successfully.

Dr. Armada taught me the value of being meticulous when it comes to finishing assignments, a lesson I've applied here and to how I react towards life generally. Dr. Armada provided me with an acute sensitivity towards every aspect of my life, not just the areas I thought were important.

I can see his influence in my life everyday. I notice everything. The commitment he required of us as students and in our work has found its way into how I choose to live my life. I am more concerned with the smaller details. I am more apt to being relentless when it comes to fitness, my diet, or my faith. I am more in tune with details when it comes to my writing.

My most memorable encounter with Dr. Armada had nothing to do with the study of communication. I don't even recall how the conversation began, but we were talking about meeting girls and being in relationships. I mentioned the anxiety I felt about meeting someone new, someone I was interested in, and how that was difficult for me. He then said something I will never forget. Dr. Armada said, *"What's the worst that can happen?"* He went on to stress that if I ask a woman for her number, she might say no, but that's the worst that'll ever happen. I will not die; there will be no great pain. And she might say yes. The benefits surely outweigh the costs.

With most risks, what you can gain is far greater than what you might lose. Chances are, you will discover that you are much stronger than you initially thought and the things you want will happen more easily. This defining moment inspired me to include here an article titled "Mr. Shy" I saved about dating. It was written by Carolyn Hax, in her news column, "Tell Me About It," on February 11th of 2000.

In her column, Hax emphasizes the notion of abandoning any fears you might have about interacting with others socially, and taking risks, which ultimately have nothing to do with partying or "alcohol consumption." While in Duluth, I trapped myself into believing that "drinking" was my ticket to building stronger relationships. I was wrong.

Carolyn advises and encourages guys to step up and talk to girls, which will lead to developing a more comfortable social demeanor and the possibility of acquiring more dates. Hax stresses the theory of numbers: that is, the more you do it, the easier it gets. Despite the fears I had about meeting new people, I began to recognize the priceless advice that it wasn't going to kill me. Thanks, Carolyn.

My most memorable lesson I learned from Tom Endres, former Chair of the Communication Department, wasn't anything about our discipline either, but of his commitment towards his family and for his students. For him, family came first. He showed me that when it came to school, work, or anything else: if your family needed you, you should drop everything else.

Besides enjoying hearing his motorcycle stories, or hearing details about his career, I learned about values and principles that gave me the foundation to live a more meaningful life. When you take risks and act from the heart, nothing is impossible. His influence furthered my appreciation for the value of personal relationships, how they move you, how they teach you, and how they benefit you.

As I found out, in the end, the professors who I have written about were meant to teach me something, and not necessarily about Christian morality, rhetorical criticism, or communication. My time at St. Thomas had to do with more than the courses I took and the education I received. It was more of a life-strengthening experience that was disguised as a list of required classes.

It's when we think we are lost, that we often get pulled back, sometimes by means we don't completely understand or necessarily accept. Tom provided the class of 2003 with a message from a Dean Koontz' character, Reverend Harrison R. White, in the book *From the Corner of His Eye*. This message offers insight to furthering one's own purpose while developing one's full potential. It is so bizarre how these inspiring messages find their way into our lives.

When I received this piece of writing, I decided to save it because one day I might want to reflect on my course with Tom. Little did I know I'd be including it in my own personal reflection, years later. It is proper and fitting to my message.

"(I)n every day of your life, there are opportunities to perform little kindnesses for others, both by conscious acts of will and unconscious example. Each smallest act of kindness—even just words of hope when they are needed, the remembrance of a birthday, a compliment that engenders a smile—reverberates across great distances and spans of time, affecting lives unknown to the one whose generous spirit was the source of this good echo, because kindness is passed on and grows each time it's passed, until a simple courtesy becomes an act of selfless courage years later and far away. Likewise, each small meanness, each thoughtless expression of hatred, each envious and bitter act, regardless of how petty, can inspire others, and is therefore the seed that ultimately produces evil fruit, poisoning people whom you have never met and never will. All human lives are so profoundly and intricately entwined—those dead, those living, those generations yet to come—that the fate of all is the fate of each, and the hope of humanity rests in every heart and in every pair of hands. Therefore, after every failure, we are obligated to strive again for success, and when faced with the end of one thing, we must build something new and better in the ashes, just as from pain and grief, we must weave hope, for each of us is a thread critical to the strength—to the very survival—of the human tapestry."

This passage isn't too terribly long, yet its message speaks volumes. Every day we are faced with extreme challenges, where we struggle between making certain choices and eliminating others. Many times, we find ourselves facing regret, sorrow, and anxiety. This is the story of my life. Everyday we witness the bad decisions others make as well as the ones we make ourselves.

I often reflect on those nineteen days in September of 1998. At any moment, my life could have taken a turn for the worse. That didn't happen, but it was always a possibility. It seemed like my accident triggered a number of negative events. Or maybe it simply gave my family and I the awareness of the truth behind what actually exists. We were just blind to the reality of a world in pain. Our society needs a renovation. This may be difficult, though, with all the bureaucratic immorality in police departments, the court systems, and other institutions.

It is heartbreaking to see what our world has become. People are abused every day. So much suffering is fueled by a lack of moral standards and faithless endeavors meant to abuse the system. I hope and I pray that justice will prevail, or at least improve, even though it may only get worse. We need to move out of the dark and into the light.

"For learning about wisdom and instruction, for understanding words of insight, for gaining instruction in wise dealing, righteousness, justice, and equity; to teach shrewdness to the simple, knowledge and prudence to the young—let the wise also hear and gain in learning, and the discerning acquire skill, to understand a proverb and a figure, the words of the wise and their riddles."

(Proverbs 1: 2-6)

U GOTTA BELIEVE

SIXTEEN

Now Me

When I began college in 1996, I was on my own for the first time. During my senior year in high school, as well as the summer before, my life seemed to have reached a new plateau. I had always developed later than everyone else my age in athletics, personal relationships, and confidence. At the start of my senior year in high school, I finally was becoming comfortable with myself and my abilities.

I would say that I made the most growth interacting with the opposite sex, even though I can still be somewhat apprehensive to this day. I had always been anxious around girls my own age. I was never sure of myself and had zero experience with the so-called "girlfriend" relationship, and to be honest, it worried me. I just wasn't ever sure if girls were interested.

The summer before my senior year began like any other, lifting weights in the high school weight room. I was improving my strength and increasing my speed. Being in the weight room not only increased my chances of playing, but it gave me an opportunity to build relationships; it was a great way for me to work on my interpersonal communication skills. So, I was in the weight room every day and it was paying off.

It was also during this summer that I became an employee at a local retail store. I worked with a few of my teammates and we soon befriended a group of girls from another town. I was finally beginning to be comfortable interacting with the opposite sex. Things were going great. I was becoming a better athlete, meeting girls, and becoming more adept at interacting socially. It was a fantastic summer.

That summer I met Kimberly, a person who has proven her unconditional love for me time and time again. I know I have a friend for life. Her commitment to my recovery can't be described; she truly was one of those angels in disguise.

During the first three years of my high school career, I would see other students with their girlfriends and I would be envious. Pretty pathetic, huh? I used to care so much about the way I looked and the way I acted that it was almost as if I wasn't being "me." I was impersonating a fake, someone who I thought was "cool." This happened pretty much from the fourth grade until I was a senior in high school.

Yes, there were always those who led and those who followed. I was always a follower, simply because I sought the approval of others, and just wanted to "fit in." I was not confident enough and was, in my mind, somewhat weak.

Much of middle school and high school was kind of a joke anyway. At least it was for me. Students were rejected, put down and treated poorly, or treated like they were royalty. It was ridiculous.

All I needed was a little confidence, which usually tends to be the case in most situations, for most people. Believing in yourself and your ability is what decides your success. It was then that I began to consider the power of belief. This became crucial in every aspect of my life, from simply living to discovering all that was possible.

When maturity sets in, you begin to see things in a new light, a new perspective. I slowly became more and more aware of what was going on with my body, and the corresponding effects that were changing in my mind. Even back then, being aware of the "core" experiences in my life was about remembering, not reminiscing about past failures. This not only strengthened my perception of myself, but also helped filter out the unhelpful false impressions I made about my life.

Consider the movie *The Karate Kid*. I am inspired by the insight Mr. Miagi offers Daniel in the movie and its sequels. Finding balance in my life was necessary for me to shape my personality. Things such as winning or losing, being rich or poor, had no influence on the possible achievements I was capable of. Losing to an opponent is one thing, but losing to myself was another. Backing down to fear and beating myself up served no purpose. It did, however, have the potential to strengthen my passion.

Losing to my own fear was a complete waste of time. I saw that it fell in the same category as letting others demoralize me by their opinion of who I was. It only mattered what I thought of myself. It is so hard to make friends and engage in fulfilling relationships, let alone be happy when the day is over. Everyone has a sense of how they are viewed by others, what others think of your personality, what others think of how you look, and what others think of how you act. In the end, it really doesn't matter.

I am not weak or arrogant. I empathize with people and their struggles. I can't tell you enough that life is too short to worry about what some person said to you or how much they hurt you. That is their loss for being blind to your true self. Maybe they will learn, or maybe they won't. But I can guarantee that if they aren't feeling a large void in their lives right now, they soon will.

It's just a matter of time, like anything. It took me a long time to realize the reality behind the value of personal relationships. Just the other day, my mom commented on how I now engage in deeper conversations with her friends. Because of my experience, I now feel comfortable around people of all ages; this is just another bonus gained from my adversity. I communicate more openly with people, without giving in to my fear of being rejected or being disliked, as I had throughout most of high school.

Richard Carlson writes in his book *Don't Sweat The Small Stuff… and it's all small stuff* many suggestions that help us lead happier lives despite the pain. There will be hard times; that's a fact, but our attitudes can change the way we see them. Life is about action, what we do when confronted by adversity and how we react to it.

Carlson notes the importance of seeing every experience through someone else's eyes; it offers us a new perspective. I love to complain about how life isn't fair and how much better my life would be if my accident had never happened. Sure, I might be physically stronger, so much further ahead, but then I consider everything I've gained because of my accident, and how my personal relationships have improved.

Everything is a step on the journey, and mine has been one of amazement and discovery. It has been both painful and difficult. I see that I was struggling. I was in a wheelchair. I was weak. I needed help. My friends were finishing college. I was stuck in therapy. But I was alive.

Always try to see the positive side of things. Look for the good things a challenge offers. My initial problem in finding these advantages was that I needed to lower my defenses and look with eyes that saw past the horror. My only option: to live for the moment, for every moment.

As I found out, tomorrow is never a guarantee. Uncertainty lies at the heart of our lives. We have no control, even though we think we do. We are simply here for the experience. I feel a strong passion to use my experience to inspire others. And we don't even have to share similar pains; my passion will offer hope.

I think people love reading and hearing success stories; it makes them feel not so alone. It made me feel not so alone. Walking a path alone is difficult, but when you have someone to walk it with, it somehow becomes simple, almost pain-free. The strength you exhibit by yourself is one thing, but when you add up a large number of people fighting the same fight, the strength is increased exponentially.

I read an article about three young men who died at the expense of another who was driving under the influence of alcohol and swerved into oncoming traffic. The mother of the young men who died spoke of forgiveness, because the driver who swerved in traffic was only human, and she realized it was a terrible mistake, a mistake that could happen to anyone; he will have a lifetime of reflection. Hearing this story made me realize that we must always keep our senses in check. In the blink of an eye, something catastrophic can happen, taking lives, and surely destroying countless others.

Of course, these events aren't always intentional, but where do you draw the line? Forever is a pretty powerful word when dealing with the life of a family member. We can't comprehend its magnitude until we realize what we've lost is never coming back. Please, keep your head on straight, and don't forget to be aware of the tragedy we encounter on our way to eternity.

And please remember, be mindful of the fact that there are no guarantees in life, and live each moment as if it were your last. Losing a loved one is undoubtedly the most heartbreaking reason to never undermine the value of our personal relationships and stay in touch with our self-discipline. Both themes, mindfulness and no guarantees, walk hand in hand, and are especially visible when tragedy occurs. There were no guarantees that I would ever reclaim my life, but it was this mindfulness that I maintained that contributed to my return. You just gotta believe.

"God made *introverts* and *extroverts*. He made people who love *routine* and those who love *variety*. He made some people '*thinkers*' and others '*feelers*.' Some people work best when given an assignment while others work better with a team."

(Warren 2002)

SEVENTEEN

People First

The Hero's Response

Dear God, I keep thinking that my life has been ruined.
So many of my hopes have been dashed.
When I look out at the future,
all I see are dead ends and "no exit" signs.
Suffering loss seems to have condemned me
to a meaningless existence.

> *Remind me that you are the God of*
> *restored hopes and new beginnings.*
> *With you, there is no such thing as a ruined life.*
> *You call me to adventure in good times and bad.*
> *Let me respond affirmatively by accepting*
> *the challenge of the hero's journey.*

I must do battle with despair and emerge victorious.
Deliver me from negativity and defeatism.

Help me to believe in miracles.
May I remember that every crisis contains
the seeds of both peril and promise.
> *You want me to respond with hope,*
> *with an attitude that never stops believing*
> *in a better life. I can only do this*
> *as I draw on the resiliency that*
> *you placed within me at my making.*
Thank you for the flow toward wholeness at the center of my life.
Because of this healing stream,
I need not be intimidated by my new circumstances.
The resources needed to deal with them are within me.
Accompany me on the adventure of finding these resources,
and the hero's journey will guide me to a better future. Amen.

—Evan Howard

I want to express my gratitude to each and every person who has stood by me throughout this experience. Recognizing the necessity of having others in my corner during this traumatic time has been so important. If I hadn't had that support, I would not have progressed as quickly, or remained diligent in my quest for a breakthrough. Having that support, having that love, gave me the strength and conviction to remain steadfast from beginning to end. Hope is what I needed; heart is what I got.

Gratitude is almost a myth these days. So many never get to appreciate the kind of caring and sharing that I received. I don't mean that people don't appreciate their lives and the things God has given them; they just haven't been at the end, or near the end, where material possessions mean nothing and people mean everything. This experience has given me more than I could have ever received had I chosen a different path home that fateful night.

Can I see my recovery as inevitable? Definitely. If I look at it any other way, I'd continue to kick my own ass, day in and day out. I'd be resentful, angry, with suicidal tendencies, unable to cope. Think about it; how many times have you found yourself angry at yourself, at the world, when you get yourself so wrapped up in everything that is not important, and will never be important, so that you can't see the true "you"?

The true me was revealed because of the circumstances I experienced. I can guarantee this new path will be the road to eternal success. My life will be an inspiration and I will influence the world positively. My life, as I see it, has always been about fulfilling that third side of the Dorito Principle, living for the common good.

While enduring therapy, I had friends visit me at Sister Kenny. I would guess it gave others a feeling of hope, an appreciation for their lives, while acting as a bridge for me. They saw me physically and mentally weak, unable to do anything on my own, without a purpose in mind except living; I offered them hope.

Everyday we see people going to work, going to church, going to the gym, doing their everyday routines, seeing the way their eyes are fixed on that one goal, knowing they have a schedule to uphold. I didn't show that focus. My eyes were glazed over, my right arm fixed at my side; I was in a wheelchair. I didn't show the motivation to start my day, or end it. I had to have a nurse shave me, brush my teeth, and wipe my ass. I was oblivious.

I was in my own little world, where it didn't matter if I was at work by 7:00 a.m. or made it to the gym by 4:00 p.m. It just didn't matter. People were genuinely interested in my recovery and how I was coping. I of course do not remember the early days, but my mother has explained them in detail. Friends felt sorrow that I had to endure this. If only everyone in therapy had a following as I had.

My situation produced a great deal of curiosity. Most people are interested in how someone undergoes such a trauma, or attempts to improve from a weak psychological and physiological condition. My rehab was interesting, creating a fascination many had never had before. It was new to me and to everyone I knew. My corner was filled with people who were other-oriented by nature, and cared about everything I was experiencing.

Being other-oriented is such an important characteristic to have as one travels such a journey. It means to "focus on others rather than only focusing on you own needs." Society as we know it is often egocentric. That is, everyone is so focused on their own needs, and their first inclinations are to serve themselves. After all, human nature is all about self-actualization and furthering one's own situation. We have bills to pay, children to feed, real life responsibilities. Or in Matthew 7:15's case, a career to protect.

The intrigue this experience created was huge. So much was at stake, both my present and my future. I soon figured out that the only way to travel such a road was one step at a time. Inch-by-inch. Brick-by-brick.

If I had rushed, my skills would not have become fully developed. Since I have always been in a hurry, taking my time with my skills was tedious; it was mind numbing. I felt time was running out. I didn't realize things take time to materialize, and that most things in life get better with age. For me, time was a godsend. I was young and hadn't lived a full life, and I wasn't too old to learn new things.

And since I was young, I was strong. Medical professionals know that if you are an athlete, your drive and commitment will work in your favor. Whereas someone else might quit, give up, or lack the proper work ethic, athletes seem to possess that inner passion, or instinct for that matter, to work extremely hard at a specific cause. Playing football in both high school and college had given me not only an experience of camaraderie, but one of severe dedication. I wouldn't quit. I would always give an extra effort, 110 percent, especially in my rehabilitation. It is, and always will be, about the journey, never the destination.

Ask yourself, "Do I possess the heart? Am I committed?" The answers are about the ability to live our lives to the fullest, without worrying about the wickedness or the unfairness we witness along our way. Many people shy away from an oncoming challenge, but a select few embrace this challenge, accept it as an unforeseen opportunity, and attack it. It is all about surrendering to that oath to become what you are meant to be.

John Maxwell exhibited this undying spirituality throughout his life. He spoke of your attitude as "the eye of your soul. If your attitude is negative, then you see things negatively. If it's positive, then you see things positively." No matter how many times I resent the fact that my accident happened and reflect on the way my integrity was violated, I still find myself searching through the bewilderment of my own psyche for the positive lessons. My life has always been about satisfying my own passion to do something more. Becoming great wasn't necessarily about increasing my bank account or purchasing a new home. And it sure as hell wasn't about popularity or gaining false friends.

Remember, nobody said life was going to be easy. Always see the opportunity in every difficulty. This attitude will build character and develop your soul. We need to view these problems we face every day as potential teachers.

Maintaining a positive attitude surely strengthened my ability to influence others by developing an other-oriented approach. Challenge your inhibitions to fight through your anxieties and become a friend to all. Like I have said before, life is and always will be about personal relationships.

Greatness is almost certain to be obtained by those who do not go quietly into the night and those who see the infinite power in developing their weaknesses, which in turn become their strengths. The Bible proclaims that all things, not just some things, are possible to those who believe. Philippians 4:13 states, "I can do all things through Christ who strengthens me." There is no reason whatsoever why we cannot live the life we crave so unmistakably. It is obvious what we are meant to do.

Jesus will walk with us, through the valley, during the storm; He will carry us during the saddest times of our life. That is the promise He made to us. Through being other-oriented in nature, we gain unimaginable wealth. Take it from me; never waste your time on anything self-serving. If you do, you'll live a self-fulfilling prophecy. I was uncertain of what that was, so I asked my professor, Bill McD.

Bill said it was "a view of the future we get into our heads and then almost cause it to happen by the attitude we have toward it. It describes someone almost talking themselves into an outcome almost happening in their lives." This works for both negative and positive experiences alike. I can think of a few times I talked myself into imagining the way an encounter would turn out, and it happened exactly how I imagined. These were, as you may have guessed, negative events in my life.

My attitude was negative. But what if I had always projected a positive attitude, a more optimistic approach toward an unfavorable situation? This would of course provide a favorable outcome, a more encouraging result. By maintaining the right attitude, a win-win attitude, we'll witness successes that will be more than we had hoped for. This is how the Bible defines faith. There are purposes in our lives that we had no idea even existed.

I have learned to have a great deal of patience since my journey began. I was under such hostile conditions, including my physical distress at Chester Creek and my intense uncertainty at Sister Kenny, and this has been, by far, the most challenging thing I have ever faced. I doubt I will ever experience a more pride-swallowing time in my life, ever. When your supporters maintain the highest level of patience towards your weaknesses, it is difficult to come away without extreme patience and compassion.

Using patience to work for the greater good of the world produces not only a feeling of gratitude, but it also gives you the most satisfying desire to continue to help others which, in turn, *helps yourself*, just as Dave Pelzer suggests. Whatever the case may be, offering yourself for the purpose of helping another human being is probably the most powerful, legitimate, and character-building experience you can have. Nobody knows how his or her life will turn out. If this is true, there is no reason why anyone should give in to his or her own self-doubt. Why not surrender to the idea of not being perfect and of making mistakes? That is how we learn, by trial and error, and how we develop a gentler soul.

Imagine how I must have felt after learning my contribution to the incident on September 27, 1998. *I am a failure. I don't even deserve to be alive. How could I have done this? I was smarter that that. I'm an idiot.* My initial feelings, however, were not true representations of reality.

Luckily, my attitude changed. It takes a strong person to deal with difficult times, but it takes an even stronger person to rise above them. For me, this usually takes seeing the world and the heartache felt by others. This, however, produces feelings of disappointment. I have been extremely disappointed in myself for gaining the least bit of comfort from someone else's pain.

But after evaluating this idea, I realize that what it produces is more of an understanding, not necessarily a satisfaction. I think appreciation is more accurate. I am more appreciative now than I had ever been before. It is impossible to put yourself in someone else's shoes without learning something about yourself in the process. So of course, I've learned a lot about myself.

Empathizing with another person's journey has been most rewarding, and it has required my walking a similar path. Yes, it was possible for me to think I could understand how someone else felt prior to my own accident. Maybe I was ignorant. Perhaps I was making generalizations. I don't know. I do know that true empathy requires having had an experience with just as much, if not more, painful feelings.

Since starting a job at a hospital, I have had multiple opportunities to gain the insight and empathy I hadn't been using. I can't even decide if I ever had it to begin with. I mean, I was always considerate and caring, but I sometimes think I was missing the understanding involved with serious illness or extreme loss. And this I attribute to the fact that I had never experienced anything remotely close to struggle and the corresponding consequences it produces.

I discovered this, or recognized it, working in the ICU at Methodist Hospital. The people on the intensive care unit, both my managers, Joanne and Faith, and fellow employees alike, took a chance on me; I had no experience, and they trained me into a position that deals with dire necessity. I hadn't realized I would be responsible for so much in a given day. Talk about a big morale booster. My confidence has risen significantly. I finally get what life is all about: being appreciative for what you have, through the good and also the bad; strengthening personal relationships; learning lessons; developing your soul; seeing the road others have traveled and feeling a sense of calmness about yours.

On October 6, 2004, I cared for an eighty-seven-year-old woman named Dorothy who was experiencing severe respiratory complications and required intensive care. When I first entered her room, I thought the nurse just needed help. The nurse asked if I'd be able to feed the patient, as she was unable. I thought nothing of it because many of the patients are elderly and are just too weak to feed themselves.

When breakfast arrived, I began to help her eat. I learned that she had diabetes, and discovered that she had two disfigured arms with no hands and that one of her legs was amputated from the knee down. I was amazed at the profound conversation this woman and I had. We spoke of college, her life, and the quality of the eggs she was given for breakfast. She had her wits about her too. She did not act a day past sixty.

This was a turning point in my life. Just the day before, I had been feeling sorry for myself because I felt I was so far behind. Dorothy enjoyed my joking demeanor and we had a really good conversation. That moment I recognized how great my life truly was and how influential others who experience far greater difficulties can be. It was definitely a wake-up call.

Working in heath care has really opened my eyes to how fortunate I am to have come away from an accident that should have crippled or killed me. Knowing this provides me with the vigor to walk through life with an attitude of relentless conviction. Embracing every revelation, and walking without an ounce of fear, gives me the courage to accomplish anything. Remember, sometimes things aren't always what they seem.

At first, I saw my glass as half-empty. It took me a few life-changing experiences to realize otherwise. The glass is, and always will be, half-full. You just have to see the big picture. All the small, trivial things we think are so important mean nothing in the end. Our looks. What we own. Our job. These don't mean much. As found in Psalm 23, my cup truly "runneth over," and as Harold Kushner suggests from his analysis of the psalm, we need to be grateful that we are alive, that our bodies work, and we have friends to "demonstrate" our "humanity" with. For these abilities, our cups "will always overflow."

This is another reason why I felt the urgency to narrate my experience. I see others benefiting from reading my personal account about adversity and the struggles I endured, how I saw through the pain and how I persevered. I want to give a little of myself to anyone who is willing to listen, or who just doesn't know exactly where to turn. This is my pledge to you.

I want everyone to be happy with who they are, regardless of what ignorant individuals think. Live for yourself. I learned the hard way, and I can't stress this enough: remember that you have choices. Make the choice to live your life by your standards, and follow your heart.

"Passion: There are many things in life that will catch your eye, but only a few will catch your heart... pursue those."
(Succesories Plaque)

EIGHTEEN

Destiny

Destiny: 2. The predetermined or inevitable
course of events considered as something beyond
the power or control of man

—*The American Heritage Dictionary*

Maybe it took this serious of an adversity to help me
clarify the big picture. Sometimes a struggle stays with a
person and never leaves. For a long time, mine controlled
my life. I hadn't been able to anticipate it and, moreover,
after it happened I was unable to predict my future.

What happened is set in stone; we can never go back
and change how we reacted, so why question ourselves?
What happened to me was out of my control. Of course,
I reflect on how I responded, but doing so only makes a
difference in how I'll live my life now and in the future.

I constantly tell myself that my future would have been
different had I acted differently in the past, but would I
really have wanted a different future than the one I have?
The lessons learned were invaluable. Maybe my life happened the way it did to encourage me to write this. Maybe

this is the way I will reach the world in a much more influential way than I would have otherwise been able. This is not just a way for me to rationalize my experience. Remember that purpose I spoke of earlier.

It's not a coincidence that I learned that personal relationships are almost as valuable as life itself, or that friends will come and go, except for a special few who will remain in your life forever. I have been blessed by meeting so many wonderful people because of this one event. My gratitude is really a genuine, profound feeling, one that is beyond boundaries and out of reach for many individuals. I am able to see the good, despite all the bad.

Fate is under severe scrutiny these days. It is difficult to know what to believe, especially since one person will tell you to follow one path, while someone else suggests another. My recommendation: find out where your passion lies and never look back. My problem is that I am one of those types who has the tendency to always look back. This has proven to be a big mistake. And not doing this is especially difficult when something as challenging as what I experienced occurs.

I've kept questioning what might have happened had I taken a different way home. What if Matthew 7:15 missed me completely? In that case, I'd have graduated from UMD with a degree in business and would not have learned about life. Surely I wouldn't have met the wealth of individuals I have met, solely because of my dire difficulties. I would not have met Anita. I would not have met Bill McD., Dr. Armada, Tom, Kim, and everyone else at St. Thomas. Or Darrel and Kristi. I would not have met Elin or Sue. I would not have met Jackie. Kelly. Angie. George. Lynette. Debbie. Wendy. Tim and Nancy. Jamie. Clint. Everybody else at Sister Kenny. Everyone at Methodist. Everyone at the Brain Injury Association. There are so many people I would not have had the privilege to meet.

God says everything happens for a reason. A few weeks prior to my accident, my mom sent me an article from the *Star Tribune*, written by Larry Simoneaux. I totally forgot about that article until my mother mentioned it one day, a couple years back. I knew it would be a great addition to *23* since it shows the significance of fate, destiny, and all that we endure. After receiving it in Duluth, I of course read it and put it along with the things that fell into the category of "things parents worry about." I didn't give it a second thought. When I read it again, for the first time since 1998, it was almost like a punch to the face.

When I first received it I, of course, was indestructible. This is a simple attitude that young, inexperienced, college students feel when they are living the good life away from parental supervision. I can't even give you an estimation of how many times I have heard my dad say *"Be careful!"* as I was walking out the front door. I didn't know how important it was to take his advice seriously.

Some people totally play down the possibility of things happening for a reason. I have heard others say, *"Well, it doesn't mean anything; it was just bad luck."* Yes, it may very well be just life happening, but it is necessary for us to learn the lessons life offers. There is no point in continuing our fearful attitude, telling ourselves how bad we have it or how hard life is.

I think maybe if I would have considered this article a little more closely I might not have valued partying so much. But, as life had it, I didn't, and decided to drink too much that Saturday night. Of course, I was there to get drunk. What a bad attitude I had. Fortunately, I didn't have to lose too much of my life to learn valuable lessons. I rehabilitated. I finished college. I thrived.

I am on a much brighter path now than I would ever have been on had this not happened. So I have to believe that this was meant to be. This realization has been my motivation to recognize where my heart lies, as it doesn't lie where I had thought. Please read the column by Larry Simoneaux and you will understand.

To the Teenagers

I don't know what it feels like to hear the words that two sets of parents received this past weekend. Like every other parent, I don't ever want to know. I'm not sure I am strong enough to handle it. So, this is to the teenagers. It's a message and a prayer. It's from us to you.

We were once just like you—just as young and daring. We were once sure our parents hadn't a clue as to what we wanted or what we were all about. We were once sure we could tackle the world. We were once, down deep, scared to death to face the world. We were once just like you.

The only real difference between us as parents and you as teenagers is a lot of "been theres, done thats." And, believe me, a lot of our "done thats" were just as dumb and silly and dangerous and exciting as anything you've done or will do. That's why we worry.

We made it through. We got older. We fell in love. We got married. We had you. That means we sat up endless nights while you were a baby. We changed you when you were wet. We fed you when you were hungry. We held you when you cried.

We watched you take your first step. We made stupid faces to see you laugh. We listened to your first words. We bragged about you at work.

We sent you off to your first day of school. We kept your drawings and school projects. We put your birthday cards on the refrigerator. We watched you in your first play. We cheered for you when you made the team. We worried about whether you'd be popular, and then, when you were, we worried about your friends.

We were angry when we shouldn't have been. We asked you questions we shouldn't have. We made mistakes and hurt your feelings. We didn't say, "I'm sorry" or "I love you" often enough. We argued with you. We laughed with you. We stayed awake in bed and worried when you stayed out later than your curfew.

We watched you change before our eyes into strong young men and women who were about to leave us. We were scared and happy and sorry at the same time.

We want to see you become firefighters and doctors and lawyers and policemen, merchants, pilots, beauticians, teachers, librarians, and forest rangers. We want to talk with you about how exciting your work is. We want to listen to you tell us how dumb or mean your boss is.

We want to see you meet the man or woman of your dreams. We want to see you fall in love and do the same crazy things we did. We want you to get married. We want to pass you a few dollars to help you through the rough spots. We want to see you have children and watch you start all of this all over again.

The thing we're most afraid of is that, sometimes, those things we worry about happen. Sometimes, for no rhyme or reason, you're taken from us by things beyond our control. Sometimes, we never get to see or do the things I've talked because you're not here anymore—and that is a hurt that cannot be described.

So, this is for the teenagers out there. It's the same thing parents have said to their children forever. It's the same thing you'll say to your children. They'll feel the same way about hearing it from you as you do when you hear it from us.

Please. Be careful.
We love you.
You're all we really have.

(Larry Simoneaux)

Can you even comprehend the impact this article had on me as I read it again for the first time since September of 1998? Initially, I thought to myself that it was just my luck to receive that article from home and then get hurt shortly thereafter. *Why did Mom have to send that? If only my parents hadn't been so worried about something bad always happening. Couldn't they just let me live my life?*

But after reflecting on the message, I became calm, calm in the sense that I finally understood how much my parents loved me. It made me consider everything that could have happened to me but never did. I felt peaceful. After reading about the two young teenagers who died after a graduation party in Washington, fear also traveled through my body. I could have died too.

The hard truth is tough to take. I don't know why those two young teens died, while I, too, was under the influence of alcohol and lived. I don't understand how it is decided that some people get a second chance while others don't. Just like *The Purpose Driven Life* says, the feeling of eternity is alive in all of us. All we have to do is get ourselves out of its way and let it find us. It lies in the depths of our souls, where our true hearts are.

Life is, after all, about personal relationships. This needs to be our most revered commitment. A plaque I was given back in 1998 gives the following advice:

> *In life what sometimes appears to be the end*
> *is really a new beginning.*

This is especially true when you face the most adverse situations, where even staying alive isn't a guarantee. Remember, there are no guarantees. Just after my accident, I kept looking at my life as close to being over, not just beginning. I felt like I was being punished. I had my share of false hopes and disillusioned ideas of how my life was supposed to turn out.

What I was seeing simply turned out to be an indispensable lesson I didn't want to accept: the power of a *new beginning*. I wanted things to go back to the way they were. But they couldn't. Many of my friends had already moved out of Minnesota, for example.

However, I was able to rekindle a few friendships that had been in the shadows. Sometimes the friends you gather are drawn toward you by fate itself. Take Steve, for example. Our friendship evolved because of my accident, and who knows if we would have developed an intimate relationship had it not happened. Yes, we knew each other prior to the accident, but we hadn't been fulfilling our commitment to our friendship until he came to visit me.

It was important for me to see my accident, like the advice in the plaque suggests, as a *new beginning*. Nobody cares about what you should have become, or what should have happened.

That makes no difference. People only care about what did happen and how you persevered. In my case I could either choose to continue to struggle against myself, regretting my losses, or, I could choose to triumph over my most difficult test.

Remember, whatever lies ahead usually turns out to be much easier than you'd expect. Everyone faces self-doubt at one time or another, but it is how we react to this doubt that provides us with a glimpse of our ability to overcome adversity. I really didn't realize when I was lying in the hospital that so many others have undergone similar injuries or disabilities, only to achieve what God has set them to do.

Why did I have see how bad others had it before appreciating how fortunate I truly was? It almost seems immoral. Why can't I see all the good in my life without making such comparisons? I need to make sense of my life, especially after receiving this attempt to disable me.

For once in my life, I feel as though I am making a difference, a real difference. The lives I will touch, and those who will touch my life, are countless. I think I have found my niche, helping others through personal relationships. These represent the foundation behind living, behind my life.

I am forever indebted to the influence so many others have given me. It truly is a reason to live. Furthermore, this realization will place me in a position that is much more advanced than even those whose life I had once envied. I am not as far behind as I had thought. I offer thanks to Kian Dwyer, whose book made me realize,

"Don't dwell on past mistakes; rather, learn from them and let them guide you toward making the right choices today."

NINETEEN

Unbridled Enthusiasm

Building my motivation was my escape, an outlet, a way to consciously surpass fears and anxieties. I witnessed countless others offer their examples of overcoming insurmountable challenges. I hope offering you everything that has inspired me as I have made the transition from being weak and mentally unstable to being focused and entirely purpose-driven provides you with the tools to develop your passion.

I was given great messages and inspiring storylines that motivated and excited me, strengthening my burning heart to step up and accept my fate. This I couldn't take lightly. What's meant to be is meant to be, and we are strong enough to complete our lives. Do not succumb to anybody, anything, except to God, who will surely lead you to greatness. Remember, God is happy when we are happy and satisfied with ourselves.

Consider the movie *The Legend of Bagger Vance*. If you haven't seen it, I suggest you see it as soon as possible. This is not just a movie about golf. It is about how losing yourself to the experiences of disaster can lead you to a profound discovery through confrontation, self-realization, and staring adversity in the eye. If you could only see the amount of harm you are causing yourself through faithlessness, in yourself, in your relationships, and in your heart. I was being faithless. This movie showed me how to leave my past in the past, despite the drama accompanying my daily life.

If we continue to focus on why we were troubled or why we were attacked, we leave very little room for self-actualization. After much reflection, I have come to realize that I couldn't get to where I wanted to be without taking a few risks. How would I know what I was made of, what I was capable of, without taking a chance, a chance to become the person I was supposed to become, the person I was meant to be? The fact is, if I didn't take the risk, I would never know. This is another one of the hurdles I face daily. I still don't take enough risks, or at least not always the right ones.

Why listen to those who critique your dreams? They really have no idea what's best for you. A song, "Standing Outside the Fire," by my favorite country artist, Garth Brooks, offers some magical insight about our potential. Its main focus is on taking risks in life, in loving relationships, or in whatever. What matters most is having the courage to take a chance.

Nothing in life comes without a price. Yes, there are those who appear to have everything given to them, but they only represent a small percentage of the entire population. And who's to say it'll last? Remember, there are no guarantees. For most of us, we accomplish the impossible through hard work, dedication, and offering the ultimate sacrifice: long hours and tough struggles.

Since I enjoy exercise, I sacrifice a good portion of my time to be at the gym, every day, every week, every month. Exercise has improved my stamina and endurance tremendously. Early on in my rehabilitation, I had to get a lot of rest. I would get extremely tired after a long day of therapy, and after being so involved in athletics, I knew that if I wanted to regain what I had lost, I'd have to continue my workouts. Starting slowly was the key. It would have been a wasted effort if I had acted as if I could just jump back in where I left off. And by realizing that starting slowly, one inch at a time, pays off, my journey continues. It is by this kind of sacrifice that I can define my life ultimately by the standards I have chosen.

So what; I have a few minor disabilities. They don't define who I am or who I will become. After graduation, I needed a change. I took a course in nursing. I got a job at Methodist Hospital. As I mentioned, I had never worked in that setting before. I had no experience. Did I deserve the job? Probably not. But I had a good interview, and the rest is history. I had my interview on a Monday and was hired the very next day. I took a risk, started slowly, and it paid off.

We all face difficult situations. And we all face hard times. And trying to change jobs, from one field that was comfortable and guaranteed to one that was entirely new and unknown, was mentally taxing. But I did it. I took a chance. It took a huge effort on my part to make such a transition. However, after months of being there, I know it was the right choice; I have learned so much and focused on strengthening my personal relationships.

The choices we make are now and forever imprinted on our souls. Some may seem huge, while others seem small, but they all possess the very real potential to change our lives. So ask yourself, when faced with a difficult choice, what will be the result if you succeed, and what will be the result if you don't? Chances are if you take the risk, there will be much more to gain than to lose.

Sometimes we may have to give up one thing to maximize something more conducive to our futures. Becoming an individual who stands out in the crowd takes an unbridled enthusiasm, one that is far and beyond what is considered average. One cannot put a value on its worth. And remember that nothing in this world is free.

Being committed is often the ultimate sacrifice. So many factors are at risk. Time. Having a family. Everyone has different interests, and different passions. When you find yours, you will know exactly what to sacrifice, what to give up, how much to give, and for how long. It may happen in the blink of an eye. It may be subtle, or it may be crystal clear, and your life will hold new meaning. You will develop an entirely new purpose, or simply add to your current one. Nevertheless, this realization will change your life, and ultimately change the face you see in the mirror.

On the other hand, if you downplay performance, pessimism sets in, and you'll make excuses. I have made my share of excuses since 1998. I said I couldn't do things because I had a brain injury. I couldn't do things because my therapists said I would have difficulty. I couldn't do things because my thinking wasn't what it used to be. I couldn't because…of this head injury. But I have overcome and accomplished every task that I didn't think was possible.

Of course, taking baby steps and not the giant leaps you're accustomed to is necessary. But that's OK. The only competition you have is with yourself anyway. So take your time, please. Do not make excuses, not for your ability, and not for yourself. We are better than that. Accept your shortcomings, and know that everyone has them and they are sometimes necessary. They make us who we are.

It is the struggles we endure during apparently impossible endeavors that will finally lay rest to any self-doubt and uncertainty we hold. God, of course, has a specific purpose for us. When I was born, my parents weren't concerned about how I would live, or for what purpose. That moment, similar to my first three weeks in Duluth, was solely focused on keeping me alive. At birth, I weighed a mere four and a half pounds. I was premature. In a sense, when I fell in Duluth, fighting for my life wasn't new to me.

I needed to visualize overcoming every negative attitude regarding my ability while turning feeble attempts into real successes. Brick by brick; that was how I overcame, one block at a time. It is done with precision, heart, and commitment.

Some things happen quickly, while others take time. But one thing is certain; whatever happens, with the right attitude, you are bound for glory. You may not always get the victory, but you will receive a feeling of accomplishment, one that nobody can take away. Christopher Reeve offers the following advice in his book *Nothing Is Impossible.*

"At some time, often when we least expect it, we all have to face overwhelming challenges. We are more troubled than we have ever been before; we may doubt that we have what it takes to endure. It is very tempting to give up, yet we have to find the will to keep going. But even when we discover what motivates us, we realize that we can't go the distance alone. When the unthinkable happens, the lighthouse is hope. Once we find it, we must cling to it with absolute determination. Hope must be real, and built on the same foundation, as a lighthouse;

in that way it is different from optimism or wishful thinking. When we have hope, we discover powers within ourselves we may have never known—the power to make sacrifices, to endure, to heal, and to love. Once we choose hope, everything is possible."

It wasn't certain that I would ever re-establish myself, or that I would ever get to a point in my life where my disabilities wouldn't be noticeable. But it's as if I am normal again. Nobody can see my hidden struggles. As a matter of fact, I myself have a hard time recognizing them. Maybe they don't exist.

Your truth doesn't lie in some ridiculous story someone else tells you about your ability or potential. The medical field offers a lot of unfitting labels, and has been proven false more than once. We shouldn't have to surrender to the beliefs of anyone but God and ourselves. If we want to be good or even the greatest, there is nothing preventing us from doing exactly that.

How are we to accomplish our dreams when we place so much emphasis on the words of another? We should never stop dreaming about what God has in store for us. Have you given up on your dreams? When I was going through therapy, I never thought I'd be doing something like writing 23. I could really only focus on one thing at a time during rehab. I was not able to multi-task because my brainpower was so limited. The ability to multi-task is another trait working at Methodist has helped strengthen.

Nevertheless, I was relentless; losing this battle wasn't an option. The only option I saw was proving the myths behind brain injury false. And now, as I write, the severity of my injuries aren't present. Do you think that is fate or luck? When I fell, I wasn't even close to being done; I had more achievements in my heart that weren't yet fulfilled. Not surrendering to these so-called failures was what fueled me during this more-than-successful rehabilitation. I can't forget what encouraged this unmistakable drive to live my life with passion offering hope to everyone else facing desperate moments.

During difficult times, we most often find solace in places we'd least expect. I have often thought about my meeting with Matthew 7:15 and his canine on the cliff in these terms.

After reading *The Purpose Driven Life,* I found that one expression stuck in my mind and helped me see why I experienced what I did and how it was supposed to strengthen me: "It's not about you. The purpose of your life is far greater than your own personal fulfillment, your peace of mind, or even your happiness. You were born *by* his purpose and for *his* purpose."

As much as I wanted to just forget the accident ever happened, I was driven to use my experiences to my advantage, helping others along the way. As I reflect on the weaknesses I dealt with and still deal with, I realize that I am supposed to use these moments. Realizing this truth after years of resentment has definitely been a rude-awakening.

No soul has an easy journey. You can hold the world by the reins, and in a split second it may crumble right before your eyes. So when you think someone has everything, remember that the world meets nobody half way, and there is strength in personal relationships. When I think back and question my lack of control, I question the authenticity of what I actually had control of.

Yes, I have regrets. But since hindsight is twenty-twenty, I can stop feeling like a complete idiot, since mistakes are the foundation behind living. If I hadn't made such mistakes, I wouldn't have learned, and I certainly wouldn't have grown. Warren says we need to accept the fact that nobody is good at everything, and we aren't required to always be the best. I had grown up expecting the best of myself, and anything less was unacceptable.

Consequently, I was setting myself up for failure and I didn't even know it. If I wanted to prevent myself from experiencing ultimate failure, I had to change a few of my attitudes and my perception of myself. Feelings of resentment, feelings of animosity, or just bitter feelings of hate contribute nothing to the life of the healing person.

Dwelling on these emotions set me up for failure. You don't need to know how to do brain surgery or to pass the law exams to know this. But giving in to these feelings is often simply less terrifying to someone who has decided to walk through the valley of the shadow of death than is recognizing that one isn't perfect.

This requires losing yourself into your deepest consciousnesses and being open to acceptance. I had to remember the trouble I had with cognitive functioning and the hard work it took to recover even the slightest ounce of dignity. It wasn't easy. I needed to keep on moving forward. By admitting my shortcomings, respecting my weaknesses, developing my passions, and realizing my strengths, I became the best I could be.

Another of Warren's most meaningful suggestions says, "When you reveal your failures, feelings, frustrations, and fears, you risk rejection. But the benefits are worth the risk." I am usually anxious. I worry, I sweat, I get nervous. But even though I am scared to death, I gain a sense of peace once I meet my goal. But still, no matter how many times I succeed, I still feel anxious, despite positively reinforcing my ability.

It is amazing how we, as fragile human beings, can strengthen ourselves by embracing our vulnerability. It's almost as if difficulties are part of our souls. During these traumatic times, when our endurance gets tested, and we are surely facing extinction we need to rely on our resilience, our elasticity. When I find myself facing decisions that influence my future, I choose to challenge my soul, and take a few risks. It's as simple as that. No excuses.

"Some of God's greatest gifts are unanswered prayers."
(Kushner 2001)

TWENTY

Becoming Me

Believing Without Understanding

Lord of love and Lord of life,
I don't always understand your ways
or events that happen in your world,
but I know I need you.
Not as a crutch do I need you,
*   but as a guiding presence that attends my way.*
My loss has confronted me with the dark side of life.
Tragedies strike. Relationships end. People die.
I am trying to accept that you allow bad things
to happen but are still good, O God.
*   This is my ongoing challenge.*
*   Increase my faith, that I may continue believing*
*   in your power and love, though you allow suffering.*
Remind me that I wouldn't want to live
in a random universe. Without laws of nature

that apply to all, chaos would reign.
I ask you not to prevent nature from hurting me,
but to guard me against hurting myself with bad choices.
*   O God, who creates everyone equal*
*   in vulnerability, may I love you for*
*   the ways you allow yourself to be vulnerable, too.*
May I worship you without having to understand you
and celebrate my blessings while I can,
for tomorrow my fortunes may change.
Grant me your grace amid these changes,
and I will serve you forever. Amen.

—*Evan Howard*

So much of life is a huge chaotic mess; people experience all kinds of problems, struggles, and difficulties. So what keeps us in check against reality and prevents us from going off the deep end? Our purpose here on earth is to use our life for something that will outlast us. Creating a legacy not only gives us purpose, it adds to our self-worth. By disclosing our weaknesses to others, we give hope, courage, and faith to the world.

So many people are just full of hatred. They go through life carrying big chips on their shoulders always talking about how life screwed them over. These people are unaware. They are hostile, and I can tell you firsthand that, as natural as it may seem, it is not productive. Nobody succeeds every time, and it is a known fact that you will fail more than you succeed. Once I accepted this, my life took on new meaning, and I didn't put so much pressure on myself. And because of this, I discovered that it was this pressure that was most likely the reason behind my lack of success.

What I went through tested my endurance. It was so ridiculously hard, and those close to me felt what I felt. While I was in rehab, I had a very difficult time holding a conversation. My brain wouldn't allow me to execute sentences smoothly. At times

I felt like a complete moron. What I thought and what I spoke weren't in balance. I couldn't hold a conversation to save my life. My brain wasn't functioning; it was working very, very slowly. Everything took longer, and took a huge amount of focus.

Feeling pathetic because my brain speed was so limited was hard. It took me longer to get things done. Menial tasks I used to do without thinking, such as eating, reading, writing, shaving—everything using my right hand—were difficult. And because of this, I really got an in-depth look behind compassion. It wasn't hard to see the beauty other people exhibited towards me. Seeing the way others acted around me and spoke to me was quite emotional.

Every nurse at Sister Kenny exhibited such beauty; Kristi, Darrel, Jamie, and Clint were at the forefront of bringing me back. One of these nurses with whom I hadn't had that much contact, was a black man named Lester. Lester treated me like I was about to re-embark on my football career. I don't remember much of our encounter, just that he asked me when I'd be ready to play ball again; that was a great feeling.

At that moment, this brain injury wasn't a part of me; it was gone. This was because a very compassionate nurse named Lester had the courage to see beyond the weak and discouraged twenty-year-old who sat in front of him. He offered me a sense of hope, one that didn't surrender to the pressures and fears of an injury that was so overwhelming. Because of Lester's compassion, I had the courage to get myself up and finish my time at Sister Kenny without an ounce of fear. Well, actually, I suppose I was scared a little.

Once I was able to drive, I exercised at a health club near my home. I had been going with my father, and keeping my workout routines fairly regular. I wasn't at the pace or ability I was accustomed to, but it was a start. My passion for the gym still existed. My godfather, Dan, had introduced this passion to me early in life. His influence proved substantial as I fought my way back. His courage in remaining diligent after a heart attack during his late twenties has influenced his life dramatically. He started slowly by walking only *one block at a time*. Knowing this caused my passion to surpass my adversity in likewise fashion. Dan is now a "fitness machine" who exercises and trains daily.

I had also known a couple of trainers who had given me advice on my weight-training program during high school. When I saw Steve, one of the personal trainers, I looked pathetic and weak, and we didn't speak. I was with my dad and my future looked depressing. I suppose I was alive and active, but I was only one hundred fifty pounds at best and talking very little. I would always let me parents do my talking for me, as I wasn't confident enough to speak for myself. When I had recovered enough to go work out by myself, I ran into Steve again. This time, we spoke. I told him I had been injured, and he simply showed concern and compassion without treating me like an idiot. I think he saw my relentless attitude.

And to someone who honored the art of fitness and weight training, his showing me respect meant everything. Most personal trainers enjoy seeing others who share a similar passion; this passion has proven invaluable. It made a critical difference in my recovery. It helped me reach certain goals at an increased rate while improving my confidence and discipline at the same time. I sleep well. I don't lay awake at night thinking about what might have been, or how my life took to a disastrous turn, in part because of my physical efforts.

When considering the effects of my traumatic brain injury, exercise was almost as necessary as medication. Working out had the capability to trigger feelings of wellness and give me positive reinforcements that helped build and strengthen my mind. Brain injury is a disease, but with the right medicine, such as exercise, it can be cured. Remember, nobody said life was going to be easy; God didn't promise this, and neither does anybody else. However, I can guarantee you'll have a healthier life if you can feel even an ounce of the pleasure I feel after I have exerted myself in the gym. Nothing compares with it.

Plus, fitness is a great mechanism for coping with stress, pressure, and depression. Whatever difficulties you may be experiencing appear less prominent after a good workout. I can't tell you how many times I've gone to the gym feeling bitter, pissed off, and unable to cope, only to leave with a new-found outlook on life. And this I owe solely to exercise.

My level of depression has considerably lowered because of it. I am out of athletics, but my passion for exercise still exists. So my advice to you is to start a fitness program immediately. Even if you have to start slowly, like the way my godfather did, give yourself time to improve and you will receive the benefits. Remember, one block at a time.

Due to the severity and extensive rehabilitation from my TBI, I was given the unexpected gift of maturing beyond my years. Many people my age are self-centered and really only see things from their own, personal perspectives. Sure, some may empathize, others may sympathize, but most don't even have a clue; they view things with tunnel vision. We can't help this.

The only thing that can change this feeling is true, unadulterated, real-life experience. That is it. We can only see things through someone else's eyes by experiencing the same feeling ourselves. We can imagine how the other person might feel, but this gives us only a limited view.

I don't mean that young people are uninformed, or lack heart. I simply mean that their experiences are usually limited and they often value things that aren't really important. Trust me, things like material possessions, job advancements, even getting married, mean little. Yes, they are important, but sometimes we think that they are too important. The things that should be recognized, such as family, friends, and humanity, aren't given the appreciation they deserve. Remember, life will always be about personal relationships and seeing the possibilities that lay before us.

While I was in therapy, all my friends were making progress in their schooling, their careers, and their futures. At that point, I was trying to further my abilities so I could start my life. Seeing this was a huge step for me. At times I felt like I had missed out, even though we were graduating at the same time, they from college, and I from Sister Kenny. What is more important, a college education, or a real-life, live or die, unadulterated education about life itself? Your answer depends on your idea of the truth and your wisdom about the value of adversity.

Maturity resulted when I released myself from my negative feelings. This has given me a reason to live without worrying about whether I should have done one thing rather than another. Being mature has given me the confidence to go against the grain without jumping on the bandwagon, and to forget about where everyone else is in comparison to me.

For me, becoming mature was about learning from the adversity I faced, and recognizing the weight I gave it. I was desperately seeking my existence after a long struggle against anger and unknowingly hating myself. I kept wondering why this happened to me. I wasn't a bad person. Why did I have to face this struggle whereas other people, disloyal and faithless people, go unpunished? It did not seem fair.

I don't think this now, though I am not now, and never will be, satisfied with my current situation. I need to want more from my life, more from myself, and more from my purpose. This is why I will leave an impact. This is the reason my injury, my entire experience, won't be in vain. There is a reason, a reason to live, to endure, and to succeed. I don't want to look back in ten years and wonder what could have been had I not stopped feeling sorry for myself.

Like everything in this world, we are bound by the simplest theory of existence. The idea that if we set out to accomplish something one step at a time we are almost certain to achieve it isn't a myth. Nothing in life is guaranteed, and everything comes with a price, whether it be financial, spiritual, or simply about time. What we aim for cannot be achieved without paying a price.

What is it that I want? What do I need to give up in order to get what I want? Figuring out the trade is simple. For myself, I want to use this experience to get for myself everything I have ever wanted and then some. It would be a shame if I expected anything less. Why shouldn't I use the experience that almost took my life for the benefit of my life? I would be an idiot if I didn't.

Very few get to go through what I went through and live to tell about it. And for that matter, I hope and pray that no one else ever has to. But that's not reality. That's not real life. It's discouraging to see that so many people go through similar experiences, or ones that are far worse, and never use them positively. This is another reason for writing, to disclose the attitude I represent, and to offer salvation to those in need.

Brain injury influences lives and causes heartbreak. I gained the maturity to see my brain injury as a minor obstacle, one I had to overcome. If I have had even less knowledge of life itself, I might have suffered worse. Having the maturity to accept this, and rise above it, gave me the courage to put it right back in hell where it belongs.

This is one experience of many in my life, and while it provided me with a number of choices, there was only one choice I could, in all honesty, accept, namely to "let it go." To forgive is to let go; letting go is for the future. After doing this, I was set free. Instead of seeing myself as emotionally raped and abused, I saw that I was given opportunities. This of course took time. But after I realized the glory and gratification it potentially held, my life advanced.

No longer would I remain a stranger to myself, for I would accept the deal of a lifetime. What can I say? I chose to follow a road that many abandon. Of course, I wouldn't get to my destination when I wanted to, but that didn't matter. Just remember, what goes around, comes around, and the glory of living depends on the one thing you have absolute control over, your attitude.

Attitude is, after all, everything. Someone can control your job, your finances, and your overall existence. But the one thing that can't be touched by another individual is how you react to life. Do you maintain a strong sense of self that doesn't give in to the pressures of others and their opinions? Are you strong in your belief, without fear of what others might say? Set your sights high and disregard negative feedback that could potentially limit your efforts. This is maturity; this is what matters most.

Never underestimate the power of your trials. Always stay true to your most profound attitude, making adjustments where necessary. The race is long, and won't be determined by any single experience. There may very well be a starting point to your journey, but there will never be an end.

"A word about limitations: limitations aren't permanent. Limitations are markers that say how far you've gone in the past."

(Strand 2003)

THE BIBLE

TWENTY-ONE

Thou Shall

Whatever inspires you, let it be your breakthrough to life. For me, I discovered a fight inside, a burning desire that wasn't found on a football field, a job, or in a weight room. It wasn't until my entire being was in jeopardy that my spirit awakened. The most significant lessons I learned became evident after seven years of figuratively defining who I was.

Music provides lyrics. Pictures give images. Movies show depictions of courage. Books feed the spirit with ideas. And writing: my writing, well, that expresses my heart. When I began to write I realized things about myself that I hadn't yet recognized. I learned that the people you have in your life, negative and positive relationships alike, are what truly matters. The job you have, and the life you lead, is nothing without the personal relationships you maintain.

You can, in a single moment, affect a life for better or worse, all by the actions you take and the hearts you touch. It isn't difficult to see how a future is graced by a single gesture of good faith. It benefits your every encounter to be more than you might be. Nobody can speak falsely about an act focused on helping another.

In the midst of chaos, a silent strength was born. Maybe it was always inside of me; it just took other adversity bearers to help it surface. I was given an opportunity, which, to the normal eye looked nothing less than like a disaster. How I managed it was where this opportunity presented itself. I didn't know if I had what it would take to overcome it, at least not from the outside. My inner spirit emerged; its dominance became evident. The courage in my heart spoke up.

The Bible expresses this level of acknowledgement in the most profound way. I never in a million years would have guessed this one experience could produce in me the passion of a lifetime. It gave me hope, desire, and an unexpected drive to become the person who saw opportunity in the face of tragedy. That is all it was, and ever will be. At first, I saw everyone else moving forward, and me standing still. It wasn't fair. I wasn't open to the fact that maybe, just maybe, I was receiving more than I had bargained for. It was a harsh reality, and I wasn't willing to accept it.

Matthew 6:34 suggests, "So do not worry about tomorrow, for tomorrow will worry about itself. Let today's own trouble be sufficient for the day." This passage spoke to me. It told me to be content with how my life was going, not to focus too much on the future, as disappointment may be right around the corner. I have not always done this, yet it is so true. It is hard advice to follow, especially when almost everything we do takes planning and organization. I had it all planned out. I was going to graduate in four years, get into business, and be successful. This was all before I had even lived and learned a few necessary lessons.

Acknowledging that I needed to slow down so I could develop myself further was hard. Of course, I thought this would surely ruin my plans. However, I found I was able to build new ones. I was able to put my faith in God, and follow His suggestions.

It was hard to decipher what was true from what was false. Nevertheless, I have learned that if you believe, if your faith is pure, there is nothing that can limit you. Read the Bible. It will make you feel better about your mission and help you live your purpose. Thou shall receive. If you listen to God, you will receive glory by placing your heart and faith where it belongs. Will you choose to trust in His power, or will you turn your back on the One who has always been there for you?

It is important to know your mission inside and out. Without this, you will be lost and search for something unattainable. It is all about having a passion that will guide you to reach your goals. Where is your passion? My passion involved writing my thoughts and feelings about the one experience I could not escape. I tried extremely hard to escape it, but the harder I tried, the stronger it got. That must have meant that I needed to champion myself and fight for everything, my integrity, my passion, my every inch.

Many people in our society simply just do enough to scrape by. For many, slowly doing the bare minimum to survive is enough. But for the rest of us, we want to achieve more and live a more fruitful life, one saturated with endless opportunity. Ralph Waldo Emerson expresses this type of attitude eloquently, when he says, "Every great and commanding movement in the annals of the world is a triumph of enthusiasm. Nothing great was ever achieved without it." As we market ourselves, nothing furthers our undying spirit except seeing ourselves through opportunities others overlook.

Mac Hammond offers many insights regarding this strategy of holding fast to your commitments. He emphasizes strongly the importance of having a positive attitude, and seeing all of life in the same way. For if you have a negative attitude, everything you see or do will have a negative spin to it. You don't want to be brought to your knees by the negativity brought on by your own self-doubt.

The book of Proverbs gives us ample hope to achieving our dreams. Throughout Proverbs, the theme of being diligent stands out; those who are quick to judge find poverty. We witness this everyday. Being diligent was my only option. I was disoriented at first, but for whatever reason I had a strong desire to make it all the way back. Proverbs 23:18 suggests, "Surely there is a future, and your hope will not be cut off." I saw diligence as the only way I could serve my conscience. Any other attempt would fuel my vulnerability.

The story of Job from the Bible is equally inspiring. Harold Kushner, in his book about bad things that happen to good people, says about Job, "The moral of the story is: when hard times befall you, don't be tempted to give up your faith in God. He has His reasons for what He is doing, and if you hold on to your faith long enough, He will compensate you for your suffering." And in Job 23, it says, "But he knows the way that I take; when he has tested me, I shall come out like gold. My foot has held fast to his steps; I have kept his way and have not turned aside" (Job 23: 10-11).

My attitude is strong; it cannot be broken or bruised by the weak attempts of my inner demons to destroy me. It would take a lot to bring me down now, especially after already conquering the one experience that was supposed to break me. This so-called disaster was actually a camouflaged opportunity. Then again, most things in life come along like this. Jobs. Personal goals. Relationships. Discovering your purpose in life. It's all in the way you see it; remember that. Attitude is everything.

Being entirely fulfilled came down to my attitude and the corresponding decisions I've made to shape my life. As just about everyone who has done the impossible will tell you, your attitude will end up being either your greatest asset or your greatest liability. For a while there, while I was feeling sorry for myself, my attitude was the worst thing about me. Fortunately, I was able to see my life through new eyes. I was able to see all the possibilities before me, as well as the nature of the obstacles I faced.

And what I have learned here is that we need to keep ourselves open to learning new ways of thinking. Believing in yourself is half the battle and committing yourself to following through is the other half; be sure to distinguish the importance of both halves.

It's funny how we end up discovering things that almost seem like they were meant to be there, like when I was working at my job and saw the *People* magazine with a picture of Christopher Reeve on the cover on the table in the break room. I just happened to see it, but it captured my attention. To me, he is the light, someone who walked through the valley of the shadow of death and said, "Hey, wait a second; I will not go quietly." He found a new cause and a burning desire inside to keep moving forward, even though the burden was so terribly heavy.

Having doubts and concerns are enough to make you abandon your cause. For me, I was scared to death to accept the responsibility of telling my story. It wasn't until I began jotting down ideas that I felt an urgency to offer whatever insight I could. The Reeve article ended with a quotation he had seen daily as he underwent his daily therapies.

This was Superman's promise to himself as he endured the pains and mental fatigue of an excruciating rehabilitation schedule. Reeve's miraculous legacy and passion for life suggests that,

"For everyone who thought I couldn't do it. For everyone who thought I shouldn't do it. For everyone who said, 'It's impossible.' See you at the finish line!"

Yes, all things are possible to those who believe. If you don't, try imagining the world without your contributions. Think about the last person who smiled when he or she saw your face, or the person whose life you changed because of your caring heart and undying love. It is possible to change the world, one inch, one brick, one baby step at a time.

Consider the life of Christopher Reeve, his heartbreaking struggle, how he dealt with adversity, and finally how he persevered over such tremendous odds to be a shining light for everyone. Keep things in perspective. Never lose hope. And don't make excuses for your shortcomings or limited ability.

Never regress in the face of minor obstacles. Just as situations can always deteriorate, they also have the potential to improve. It's never as hard as you initially imagine; it normally takes a little longer than expected, but the end result will prove bigger. That's just the way things happen.

I have come up with a few affirmations to say if you find yourself wallowing in self-defeat and disobeying your heart.

- I will not define my life by someone else's standards or opinions.
- I will seek out positive personal relationships.
- I will not give in to the threat of self-pity, regret, or resentment.
- I will not feel sorry for myself.
- I will always have a positive attitude towards my life.
- I will forgive those who trespass against me.
- I will not abandon giving myself entirely to my cause.
- I will not follow the paths of deceit or unfaithfulness.
- I will never apologize for anything that is out of my control.
- I will honor myself and provide meaning to the lives of others.

By following these simple suggestions as you start your life anew, you'll succeed in achieving your goals, as long as your attitude stays intact and your heart never dies. So move forward.

"Faith is determining to trust God when He has not answered all the questions or even assured a pain-free passage."

(Dobson 1997)

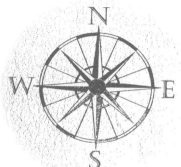

TWENTY-TWO

Vision

Struggling with confidence has always controlled me, to say the least. If you consider how much time I spent thinking and worrying about how my life should have been, or how I should have handled certain situations differently, it's no wonder that I have resented myself. *My life should have never taken this disastrous turn. I should never have been so careless.* What a waste of time.

Life is like a football game, running an offensive series to score. And as we all know, not every offensive series is guaranteed. Therefore, we have to play a little defense. We will sometimes be scored against, at which point we often find ourselves behind, struggling to stay alive. Life is no different.

We can cope, though. We can further our understanding. We are able to accept the inevitable and conquer our fate with an indomitable spirit of heart, love, and perseverance. It's a matter of being strong in mind. Can you change your mind-set from one of self-pity to one of opportunity? *Feeling sorry* for myself limited my ability to make progress, especially during the days after my accident when I wasn't aware of my purpose to serve.

Accomplishing things such as relearning to walk, strengthening my fine motor skills, or slowly getting comfortable with "Nick" again, was meaningful. I was told I would have a hell of time going back to school, let alone earning a college degree. But I felt it was necessary. It wasn't crucial to survival; however, gaining an education would benefit my integrity and my character. I needed it to grow.

And even small successes depended on the attitudes I held as I walked this road with myself. Few people get the opportunity to say that they walked through the valley of the shadow of death, were at the end of the road, and chose to follow the detour to the very end. And for many, well, they never really seem to reclaim their lives.

This small percentage of risk takers, those who say they are still in it, still in the game, who see the calmness after the storm, reclaim their lives with enthusiastic passion. Those who never say never always see the opportunity despite all the insanity. This is where we adversity-bearers begin, where others say the impossible is certain and glory is unachievable. Forget about the impossible; define the moment for yourself.

My vision is for a better appreciation of myself. By taking an in-depth look into my deepest thoughts and my innermost fears, I can limit, if not destroy, the negativity I place upon myself. I don't need to blame myself continuously for the heartaches of my past.

At this point, I feel responsibility must be taken. Matthew 7:15 should have owned up; he didn't. I accept my responsibility for being drunk, for running, for everything. But that happened in 1998. Time has passed. I need to move on. As difficult as that may be, it's crucial to developing my soul. I don't have to be happy about it, but on the other hand, I don't have to be a complete pain in the ass either. I have been resentful towards my parents for not protecting me, as if they ever could have. So I'll say it again: the past is best left in the past; there is no place for it in the future.

After reading Dr. Phil's *Self Matters*, I realized that if this is the worst thing that ever happens to me, then my life is pretty close to great. Dr. Phil writes about how we need to generate our own strength from the struggles we endure, and that we shouldn't even begin to downplay how truly bad it was. Dr. Phil offers the following suggestion, and it definitely contains words to live by as we move forward:

> "Everybody is nervous about different aspects of life. Everybody has self-doubt; everybody has fear; everybody has anxiety. But if you passively accept the excuses of your own self-talk, if you let it speak to you unchallenged, you will cheat yourself and everyone else in your life."

I was actually believing the negative thoughts I was telling myself. *I can't do it. My memory is bad. Why would she want to date a guy who talks funny? How can I be so dumb?* So many negative thoughts, and I was believing every one of them. I was cheating myself of an enduring future. My attitude sucked. My confidence was low, and it was influencing my life poorly. One of Dr. Phil's chapters starts with a quotation that puts my negative self-talk into perspective. Dr. Phil quotes Carlos Castaneda, who gave the following advice:

> "We either make ourselves miserable, or we make ourselves strong. The amount of work is the same."

In some respect, it would be harder to bring myself down continuously rather than to motivate myself up. I'd constantly have to tell myself I wasn't any good, and make myself miserable. Before my recovery, it seemed that everyone believed me when I said I was fine: "*I am OK. I am good. Don't worry.*" But it was as if it were one big lie. In reality, I wasn't happy; I had thoughts that things might have been better if I would just be dead, gone forever. Was this me? Was I a fake? I now see that all of this negative self-talk took a lot of effort.

So many people face far worse problems, and so many people get much tougher results. What do I have to be spiteful about? I can walk. I can talk. I can work. I can hear. I can see. I can do anything I want. I can do all things through Christ who strengthens me. Possibilities are available. This was my problem; I wasn't recognizing all that was there and how much I could give of myself.

So I've made the choice to use my experience as a stepping-stone to make my future better, a suggestion Dave Pelzer gives in *Help Yourself.* I know this wouldn't happen overnight. I'd be a fool if I thought otherwise. Trust me; take it from a fool. It was time for acceptance and a time to leave whatever regrets or disappointments I had behind. I couldn't allow regret to run my life any longer.

I read a suggestion from Pastor Mac Hammond, from his daily *Winner's Minute* series, that spoke of having a vision.

This excerpt spoke of how being a visionary helps you achieve your dreams. If we could start standing up for ourselves and believing the truth behind our purposes, we would soon find ourselves building lives based on integrity, hope, and value. Hammond said,

"Visionaries boldly appeal to anyone and everyone to get on board with the vision. They talk about it, write about it, and burn white-hot for it. They are future-oriented and full of faith to believe the vision can be achieved if the dream is pressed toward with enough desire. If told their dream is impossible, that just adds fuel to the fire in their spirit. They carry the vision. They cast the vision. They draw people into the vision, and they'll give their lives to see it fulfilled."

I plan to implement my vision through the publication of *23*. I want to offer what I have been blessed with learning to those who find comfort in reading about personal triumph, beating the odds, learning lessons, and the true nature behind adversity.

There is so much I have to offer. Why waste my life due to a lack of confidence, or worse yet, a lack of heart? Be sure of your ability and leave nothing to chance. Follow your vision to its completion, and always—and I mean always—give it a champion's effort. For anything less will be half-assed and lack substance. Never underestimate the power of your actions. Your faith and your attitude will ultimately lead you into greatness. And to conclude this idea, I'd like to quote a passage from Dr. Phil's book that truly defines the purpose of living.

"You cannot play the game of life trying not to lose, trying to play it safe. You must live to win."

Give it everything you've got. Dr. Phil also offers a small anecdote I found to be necessary in strengthening my own vision.

"Why in the world would you give your power away to some random "beholder"? So some boy or girl in school did not think you were cute and funny and worthy of dating, so what!"

As simple as this may sound, it is difficult to get past our inner inhibitions and feelings of rejection. But dwelling on them is a waste of time. So certain individuals had negative perceptions of who I was, and thought that I deserved harassment. I was wounded because of this perception. It wasn't the end of the world, though, and it pretty much just showed their ignorance.

Maybe they'll change, maybe they won't. Whatever they do, I am who I am. I am not going to give away the best I have because of some stereotype. If I did this, others would get the best of me. I cannot allow that; I choose to live differently.

After my first social worker at Sister Kenny suggested that I spend my life in a nursing home, a vision of triumph slowly emerged. I wasn't ever going to a nursing home; this was the beginning of the rest of my life. You see, in my heart, I had already decided how strong I was, that my vision wasn't about to be put down. It took an experience like this to make me aware of the potential of my life. As I said before, so many positives have resulted from this one negative event.

From St. Luke's to Sister Kenny to Courage Center to Normandale Community College to the University of St. Thomas, one lesson stands out: always maintain an undying vision to live for the common good. Yes, this is the third principle of Bill McD.'s infamous Dorito Principle.

Those I have met because of my accident have shaped and molded my life, helping me to fulfill the final and most important side of the dorito. My vision is simple: to use these small, yet severely important moments of shared greatness for the benefit of the world and everyone I encounter. There was a reason this happened; there is an obvious purpose. What I do with it now is up to me.

Nobody, not some overly confident police officer nor an insensitive social worker, believed in such a future for me. But it was in the cards this time, and I shaped my future through vision, faith, purpose, and heart. My vision represents a life that wouldn't give in to the petty adversities that seem to destroy the lives of so many. What it takes to maintain this adamant vision is nothing less than perfection.

I needed to come to a few realizations about myself before I could move forward. First, I needed to recognize the love my parents give me is unlimited, and also that they have helped strengthen my positive attitude. It is because of them that I am who I am; they taught me values like compassion, dedication, and maintaining a strong sense of self. I didn't understand this at first.

And second, if I am unhappy, that's my fault. Happiness is a state of mind; if I let one pathetic attempt destroy me, then I might as well give up right now. And if that's the case, I am not nearly as strong as the image I portray.

And finally, my family only cares about my health and happiness, and if I continue to feel bitter about this, I haven't learned a damn thing. The following Serenity Prayer describes this attitude perfectly:

"God grant me the serenity to accept the things I cannot change, courage to change the things I can, and wisdom to know the difference."

It took me a while to recognize that wisdom, but it came. Life as we know it is made up of our everyday experiences and the accomplishments we manifest. At first, I constantly asked my parents, "*Why?*" as if I thought they could give me a reasonable answer. It wasn't necessarily an easy question to answer. In many respects, they were more distraught than I was. We all thought I didn't deserve this. I was dissatisfied with the idea of "me," who wasn't a criminal, who was compassionate, but injured at the hands of someone who was supposed to serve and protect.

But after years of trying to resolve my inner conflict, I had a revelation. Maybe this was all part of His plan. Perhaps it was meant to fulfill my genuine purpose. It wasn't until I began visiting a couple of local churches, Mac Hammond's Living Word and Leith Anderson's Wooddale Church, that I began to consider the question I never thought I would ask, "Why not?"

Who am I to say that I didn't deserve this? Who am I to say that this never should have happened? Who am I to place blame on someone who simply made a bad judgment call? The fact is, in one sense I did deserve this, it happened for a reason, and I take as much of the responsibility as anyone. It has benefited me. I see that now.

My vision is much clearer, more developed, and stronger than it would have been without my accident. Where would I be, and what would I be doing, if I had chosen a different route is beside the point. This experience has given me more insight and more belief and I can't honestly say that I'd be just as strong today without it. It has made me who I am.

It has given me a vision I'd never even considered, or even imagined, prior to the day my journey began. Mine will be a purpose-driven life that not only satisfies the lessons of the past and present but hungers for the future ones as well. Complementing my idea of vision, Mac Hammond quotes Tom Peters who has said,

"Good business leaders create a vision, articulate the vision, passionately own the vision, and relentlessly drive it to completion."

Being passionate about your cause simply adds fuel to the fire. It makes it stronger, brighter, and more lasting. We need to realize failing does not mean that our lives will conclude negatively. Always remember what F. Scott Fitzgerald said,

"Never confuse a single defeat with a final defeat."

Ultimately, risk-taking is certain, as is believing in yourself. And see things to the end. There is no point in giving a half-assed effort, because that's the probability. It is only half-assed and you'll only get half-way to where you need to be. Going all the way is necessary. Leave no doubt. I have, and always will, have a future shining as bright as the crisp full moon we see when we walk during our most troubled times.

A favorite parable of mine is titled "Footprints." I would imagine you've most likely heard it. This short story has offered me inspiration and I hope it will inspire you.

Footprints

One night a man had a dream. He dreamed he was walking along the beach with the Lord. Across the sky flashed scenes from his life. For each scene he noticed two sets of footprints in the sand: one belonging to him and the other to the Lord.

When the last scene of his life flashed before him, he looked back at the footprints in the sand. He noticed that many times along the path of his life there was only one set of footprints. He also noticed that it happened at the very lowest and saddest times in his life.

This really bothered him and he questioned the Lord about it. Lord, you said that once I decided to follow you, you'd walk with me all the way. But I have noticed that during the most troublesome times in my life there is only one set of footprints. I don't understand why when I needed you the most you would leave me.

The Lord replied, my precious, precious child, I love you and I would never leave you during your times of trial and suffering. When you see only one set of footprints, it was then that I carried you.

—Author Unknown

How do you envision your future? I needed to create a vision to seek, define, own outright, and then finish. Nobody can give this to us. It must come solely from the desire found in our hearts. This was my problem; I hadn't been following my heart.

After coming to terms with who I am, I've recognized that my passion resides in strengthening my personal relationships, and helping others realize that just because they may have been knocked down once or twice, the game isn't over. The final bell hasn't rung yet; there is still time left. Why not use it to your advantage? If you don't, you are limiting yourself and giving your strength away.

I believe Shakespeare said it best: "*this above all: to thine own self be true.*" I wish you the best in achieving your dreams. Just be sure to recognize that being true to yourself is definite, and that sometimes defeats are necessary. Be consistent. Be relentless. Just be yourself.

"It's one thing to have a vision. It's another thing to have a sound strategy for making that vision a reality. Some leaders have the God-given ability to break an exciting vision into achievable steps, so an organization can march intentionally toward the actualization of their mission."

(Hammond 2005)

TWENTY-THREE

To Be Continued

Impossible Possibilities

O God of redeemed yesterdays and bright tomorrows,
I need a miracle.
Nothing less will do in this situation.
You have done it before, Lord.
When I look back and see your hand of blessing upon me,
I give thanks.
> *You have always provided enough work to keep me busy,*
> *enough health to keep me strong,*
> *enough love from others to keep me sane.*
Perform one more miracle in my life, I pray.
I ask not that you would change my circumstances
but that you would change me.
Awaken my heart and fill it with new life.
Instead of fear, grant me faith; instead of anger,

Understanding; instead of guilt and depression,
grace and peace.
Allow me a glimpse of tomorrow.
May it be a glimpse of life at its best.
Only you can take me beyond what is to what can be.
As you helped me to survive a terrifying crisis,
so may I help others who find themselves
in the dark night of the soul.
Sunsets and waterfalls and rainbows
are miracles of your creation, O God.
Make me a miracle, too, as I share
with the world the compassion and hope
you have shared with me. Amen.

—*Evan Howard*

The last twenty-two chapters depict my experience and how I finally found myself after years of struggle. I began somewhere between the person I should never have started to be and the man I am today. Hopefully, you were able to see how I endured heartaches and my failure to survive, or thrive, and how I overcame these. And I have described how, as I built a stronger relationship with God, His purpose for me became clear. Because of my own self-realizations, and with a little help from a number of true angels, I was able to see the glory of life, and became encouraged to help others do the same. Give and you shall receive.

Brain injury results in extreme uncertainty; but mine undoubtedly was supposed to benefit me forever. It has. I am able to apply the lesson I've learned to my cause everyday. It's one thing to recover from injuries that produce subtle differences in your life, but it is totally another issue to have things so disorganized in your life, that you can barely tell truth from trickery. A traumatic brain injury, as I have discovered, is like nothing else.

And no two head injuries are ever the same. They are dependent upon so many factors: age, sex, health, not to mention unseen characteristics such as heart, love, and self-will.

These unseen characteristics separate success from failure. It wasn't until I stopped feeling sorry for myself that my passion evolved. I would not succumb to the fears, or the pains, produced by my most devious opponent. The solemnity of this challenge was nothing to dispute. The powerlessness proved substantial; however, when juxtaposed with my heart, it became mine—I owned it.

As I have already mentioned, throughout my journey I wasn't able to plan my next move since so much seemed at stake. But then again, in the wake of this uncertainty, what actually formed was a declaration of my newfound appreciation of the glory in the kingdom of God. The only thing I knew for sure was that my faith was strong, and that in itself was enough to carry me through.

My story is just like the story of the man walking along the beach with the Lord. Sometimes we must rely entirely on faith alone; when our abilities are being tested, our heart is our only map. So never question the presence of God when you are following your heart and working diligently towards your purpose. He carried me through everything.

Finding inspiration must come directly from within, from your strong feelings of courage to a back-shivering reminder of what could have, and should have, been. Reality told me I should have died; reality said it would be impossible to live fully.

I am sick of hearing about how someone is unable to cope because a tragedy happened or because life put them on a rocky journey. I don't think people are weak because they have succumbed to such feelings or had such negative experiences. What I am talking about is much deeper. It includes developing our inner passion to help ourselves manage life without losing too much of ourselves in the process. We are capable of making sure our mental health is good enough to function everyday.

I met with two different psychologists at Sister Kenny, and honestly, they really didn't offer me solutions to coping with my losses and struggles that I didn't already know. When I met with Mike, we resolved nothing, at which point he said there was no point in us meeting if my heart wasn't there. And he was right; my heart wasn't there. I was having a difficult time heeding any bit of advice from our time together. I will say that there was one thing I keep in my daily planner to this day that was a breakthrough in our relationship, though.

Mike wrote on the back of one of his business cards three important phrases I needed to acknowledge if I was to move forward. He wrote,

1. *Be aware of negative thoughts about speech.*

2. *Challenge thoughts.*

3. *Practice speaking when self-conscious.*

This was the biggest, most profitable thing I took from meeting with a licensed psychologist, three simple phrases. When I consider how difficult a time I had speaking, I see that the insights were invaluable. I wonder how much each session cost throughout my time at Sister Kenny. It was probably expensive, and I got three basic phrases I could apply to my life. Seems ridiculous, huh? On the other hand, maybe those sessions just taught me to follow my own instincts and intuitions; if so, then of course they were worth every penny.

After being introduced to Dave Pelzer on Oprah's television show, and after buying his books, I found a message, his message, that truly inspired me to change my focus without looking back. What Pelzer taught me is by far, the best thing

I was ever given after I "graduated" from Sister Kenny. I spent $21.95 to gain an appreciation for my life, and learned I wasn't alone, that others had walked similar paths. And he's not even a psychologist. Go figure.

Throughout this, my character developed and strengthened. At least I was able to develop character. It's worth something. It cannot be taught or bought. Learning lessons and building myself up gives me the most gratifying feeling. When we understand the lessons we are taught, and as we see ourselves getting stronger by the day, we develop a sense of achievement.

Discovering ways to manage my fear has been just about the biggest hurdle I've faced. I had to search long and hard for the strength to overcome this. Despite my worst fears and all of my weaknesses, I had a responsibility to uphold. I figured if I was ever going to put this behind me, something had to change. Nick had to change, the good and the bad.

As much as part of me wants to never think about my accident and rehab again, I know that that is not reality; that is not me. I suppose knowing that it will never get the best of me ever again is the most I can expect. So why shouldn't I use it? Matthew 7:15 and the city of Duluth will remember our little encounter for days to come. Hopefully everyone has learned something about treating people fairly so an episode like mine never gets repeated.

Students have already died from the city's lack of willingness to protect everyone from Chester Creek. Beware of your safety hazards. I hope to God you can change them. The reality of it is that the city is probably still the same. It will always have my battle on its conscience, and I will tell my story in order to serve others.

Once I faced reality, my feelings about the city became less vengeful. And after Ezekiel 25:17, my family, and I accepted the loss in court, we regained our composure, and triumphantly recognized our victory was my future, which was inevitably placed out of criminal hands and back into the soft and supportive hands of our Maker.

Everyone who has been with me since the 27th of September, 1998, knows I am a better man for experiencing this adversity, and I am truly sorry for the pain it caused. I must thank you for your courage, and for guarding my back as I accepted this challenge. Your love and compassion gave me strength to achieve resilience. You are the true definition of heart, and I could not have done this without you.

The love that began in the ICU at St. Luke's is still alive in me today. In fact, I think it has built a home there and in the lives of every person I encounter. What can I say? This is my purpose.

I was knocked down, but I got back up. I wouldn't quit, especially on myself. I found out what I was capable of while getting to know some important characteristics about myself in the process. As much as anger consumed me, I found out a critical uniqueness that is common to all. Sometimes we find ourselves blaming and accusing others for influencing our lives so much that we overlook both the message and what the message was supposed to teach us.

Mistakes happen. We forget the truth that anything is possible with the right attitude. Believing in yourself, being diligent, and never giving up helps things work themselves out. Maybe it was inevitable that I was hurt. I had to go through this pain to show others how it is done, and to lead by example.

I was introduced to a couple of life-altering passages when my future was uncertain and my attitude crushed. One was written by Leo Rosten, the other is a speech by Vince Lombardi. These passages represent everything worth fighting for, and subsequently everything worth dying for. Rosten writes,

"In some way, however, small and secret, each of us is a little mad…everyone is lonely at the bottom and cries to be understood; but we can never entirely understand someone else, and each of us remains part stranger even to those who love us…it is the weak who are cruel; gentleness is only to be expected from the strong…those who do not know fear are not really brave, for courage is the capacity to confront what can be imagined…you can understand people better if you look at them—no matter how old or impressive they may be—as if they are children. For most of us never mature; we simply grow taller…happiness only comes when we push our brains and hearts to the farthest reaches of which we are capable…the purpose of life is to matter—to count, to stand for something, to have it make some difference that we have lived at all."

Vince Lombardi, the famous coach of the Green Bay Packers, in a stirring speech he once delivered, offers a similar message.

What It Takes To Be #1

Winning is not a sometime thing; it's an all the time thing. You don't win once in a while; you don't do things right once in a while; you do them right all the time. Winning is a habit. Unfortunately, so is losing.

There is no room for second place. There is only one place in my game, and that's first place. I have finished second twice in my time at Green Bay, and I don't ever want to finish second again. There is a second place bowl game, but it is a game for losers played by losers. It is and always has been an American zeal to be first in anything we do, and to win, and to win, and to win.

Every time a football player goes to ply his trade he's got to play from the ground up—from the soles of his feet right up to his head. Every inch of him has to play. Some guys play with their heads, that's O.K. You've got to be smart to be number one in any business. But more importantly, you've got to play with your heart, with every fiber of your body. If you're lucky enough to find a guy with a lot of head and a lot of heart, he's never going to come off the field second.

Running a football team is no different than running any other kind of organization—an army, a political party or a business. The principles are the same. The object is to win—to beat the other guy. Maybe that sounds hard or cruel. I don't think so.

It is a reality of life that men are competitive and the most competitive games draw the most competitive men. That's why they are there—to compete. To know the rules and objectives when they get in the game. The object is to win fairly, squarely, by the rules—but to win.

And in truth, I've never known a man worth his salt who in the long run, deep down in his heart, didn't appreciate the grind, the discipline. There is something in good men that really yearns for discipline and the harsh reality of head-to-head combat.

I don't say these things because I believe in the 'brute' nature of man or that men must be brutalized to be combative. I believe in God, and I believe in human decency. But I firmly believe that any man's finest hour—his greatest fulfillment to all he holds dear—is that moment when he has to work his heart out in a good cause and he's exhausted on the field of battle—victorious.

Pretty powerful words, huh? They describe how we apply ourselves to becoming faithful people, people who are morally good, honest, and kind; people who are strong and courageous. This describes who I will become; this is who I am, a man personifying the ability to maintain positive personal relationships through expressing the following attributes: honesty, optimism, and authenticity. I can't try to be someone I am not. I've tried different approaches to living in the past, however, what I've learned is to be "me" is more than enough.

I learned from living through rehab the value of heart and the importance of those things we can lose in life. This is especially difficult when you feel self-pity, and you find yourself with a negative attitude. But after embracing your situation, you begin to see the truth. So many others helped me get my life back. So many others gave a little of themselves to me during my most trying moments. This is where I would build my life. Not in a damn job or a college football career. Some guys build their entire lives on past glories. And sometimes they are given a false sense of their abilities.

When I look back to every person who gave me my life back, I pray they feel as much if not more glory in their efforts as I do in mine. They are the real heroes. They didn't back down from this challenge and made a valiant attempt to rehabilitate me. Hard work with a fearless attitude is like a piece of steel, unbendable.

Figuring out my new self helped me get past feelings of suicide and doubt. I didn't want to accept the person I had become because I wasn't sure where he ought to be. I felt disgraced about my condition, an attitude typical of people with traumatic brain injuries. In a split second, you lose everything and find yourself battling things you took for granted a few months before.

Yes, I was disappointed in myself. But so many people took the huge task of rehabilitating a young man who was told his chance of living was slim to none. It is my devout responsibility to announce this message to the world:

Anything is possible with the right attitude.

And when I was at St. Luke's Hospital and Abbott Northwestern Hospital, I learned something crucial. Never rule out a comeback when you're dealing with someone who never let a single moment define his life. Any lack of hope I encountered at St. Luke's or elsewhere fueled my inner spirit to do the impossible. I have to thank everyone who doubted my abilities, because if you hadn't doubted me, I wouldn't have had an inclination to do something about it.

Without some doubters, I might not have been so relentless. Maybe that was their intention from the beginning, to get me motivated. I never realized how good I had it until everything was gone. In life, there exists a small margin for error, a matter of inches. And these inches are everywhere for the person who is willing to fight for every inch.

I have also realized that there exists a select few who will do anything for that inch, whereas others will not. They are the ones who can remain in their cushiony comfort zones. Let them lead mediocre lives. I cannot do this; I have too much to give. I am finally mindful of my purpose; I am mindful of everything I can contribute. I can't be hostile about being ruled out at the beginning, because I know how terrible my condition was. As a result, I decided I would be proactive towards my life and what I was supposed to do and become. In the beginning I had to ask myself if I was worth fighting for or worth dying for.

I didn't quite yet understand how "Nick" was supposed to live, so I learned. I healed. I improved. As I said, I was unaware at first: my mind was transparent. I eventually saw many of my friends come and go. That's OK; I probably would have done the same. But after experiencing this entire messed-up attempt to define who I was, my belief system has changed. No longer will I follow the group or join the bandwagon.

My "new" self is about strengthening my personal relationships and building my life not on what others have already established, but on the images of my heart. This goal has allowed me to develop a stronger other-oriented approach: life's really about satisfying our own needs through fulfilling someone else's. Was it all part of His plan? Could I have achieved this alone, that is, without meeting Matthew 7:15 early that Sunday morning?

And maturity is, without a doubt, the most fundamental quality one should expect to acquire after such an experience. This allowed me to see the world with a newfound awareness about my losses, and to come to terms with everything I gained. This is where I was disillusioned; I had been impervious to the gains. I had been misconceiving the status of my life from the beginning. Maturity led me to realize how much I truly loved my family and to recognize their positive influence throughout and since my rehab.

I've considered why I was so intent on criticizing myself. Was it because I knew I was smarter than I showed that night in Duluth? Remember, school was never the issue. It was my extra-curricular efforts that were unstable. I was too focused on getting the approval of my peers who supposedly had the "right idea" of how to live. I shouldn't have been so worried about whether or not so-and-so thought I was worthy of friendship; it just wasn't worth it.

I've decided that no matter how much I'm beaten, or how many times I'm ridiculed, I will not give up; I am relentless.

The final lesson learned here is to never base your life on someone else's view of how you should live, or what they think your purpose should be. There are too many unknowns out there, too many uncertainties. Life can change in an instance, whether or not you give in to peer pressure or jump on the bandwagon. But it is better to stand for yourself.

Never underestimate the power of belief, and always be sure to place your focus where it rightfully belongs, on the significance of perseverance, heart, and personal relationships. And always be sure to leave footprints in the sand while you're standing outside the fire. God bless.

"Be willing to swap a temporary inconvenience for a permanent improvement. For our light affliction, which is but for a moment, is working for us a far more exceeding and eternal weight of glory."

(Brown Jr. and Brown 2000)

References

Albom, Mitch. 2003. *The five people you meet in heaven*. New York: Hyperion.

Albom, Mitch. 1997. *Tuesdays with Morrie*. New York: Doubleday.

Bast, Mary R. "Crisis: Danger & Opportunity," http://www.breakoutofthebox.com/crisis.htm.

Barnes, John A. 2005. *John F. Kennedy on Leadership: The Lessons and Legacy of a President*. New York: Amacon.

Beebe, Steven A., Susan J. Beebe, and Mark V. Redmond. 2002. *Interpersonal Communication: Relating to Others*. Boston: Allyn and Bacon.

Bird, Larry. 1989. *Drive: The Story of My Life*. New York: Doubleday.

Brown Jr., H. J., and Rosemary C. Brown. 2000. *Life's Little Instructions from the Bible: Ancient and contemporary wisdom to fuel your faith and empower your life*. New York: Testament Books.

Brussat, Frederic. "Spirituality & Practice: Resources for Spiritual Journeys," http://www.spiritualityandpractice.com/films/films.php?id=3708.

Burton, Tim, dir. 2004. *Big Fish*, DVD. Culver City, CA: Sony Pictures.

Canfield, Jack, Mark V. Hanson, and Les Hewitt. 2000. *The Power of Focus: How to Hit Your Business, Personal and Financial Targets With Absolute Certainty*. Deerfield Beach, FL: Health Communications Inc.

References

Carlson, Richard. 1961. *Don't Sweat the Small Stuff... and it's all small stuff: Simple Ways to Keep the Little Things from Taking Over Your Life.* New York: Hyperion.

Cassavetes, Nick, dir. 2004. *The Notebook.* DVD. Los Angeles: New Line Cinema.

Dobson, James. 1997. *In The Arms of God.* Illinois: Lyndale House Publishers, Inc.

Dwyer, Kian. 2005. *Living Your Chosen Eulogy: live today how you want to be remembered.* Edina, MN: Beaver's Pond Press.

Gibson, Mel, Dir. 1993. *Man Without a Face,* DVD. New York: Warner Home Video.

Gliatto, Tom, Samantha Miller, Michelle Tauber, and Jason Lynch. "Incredible Journey: Facing tragedy, Christopher Reeve inspired the world with hope and a lesson in courage." *People,* October 25, 2004.

Gumbel, Bryant. "Kyle Maynard." HBO: *Real Sports,* 2005.

Hammond, Mac. Mac Hammond Ministries. Winner's Minute. (2004, December 8). http://www.winnersminute@winnersminute.org

Hammond, Mac. Mac Hammond Ministries. Winner's Minute. (2004, October 18). http://www.winnersminute@winnersminute.org

Hammond, Mac. 2004. *Enduring Adversity: Keys to Staying Steady in Tough Times.* CD. Mac Hammond Ministries. http://Mac-hammond.org.

Keith, Kent M. 2003. *Do it Anyway: The Handbook for Finding Personal Meaning and Deep Happiness in a Crazy World.* San Francisco, CA: Inner Ocean Publishing.

Kershner, Irvin, dir. 1980. *Star Wars Episode V: Empire Strikes Back.* DVD. Century City, CA: 20th Century Fox.

King, Jr., Martin. 1974. *Loving Your Enemies.* A.J. Must Memorial Institute: Essay Series.

King, Steven. 2000. *On Writing.* New York: Pocket Books.

Koontz, Dean. 2000. *From the Corner of His Eye.* New York: Bantam Books.

Kubler-Ross, Elisabeth. 1997. *On Death and Dying.* New York: Scribner.

Kushner, Harold. 2003. *The Lord is My Shepherd: Healing Wisdom of the Twenty-Third Psalm.* New York: Anchor Books.

Kushner, Harold. 2001. *When Bad Things Happen to Good People.* New York: Quill.

Landers, Ann. 1999. "Meant Well Parents." *Star Tribune,* November 17.

Mackay, Harvey. 1988. *Swim With The Sharks Without Being Eaten Alive*: New York: Fawcett Columbine.

Maynard, Kyle. 2005. *No Excuses: The True Story of a Congenital Amputee Who Became a Champion in Wrestling and in Life*. Washington, DC; Regnery Publishing, Inc.

McGraw, Ph.D., Phillip C. 2001. *Self Matters: Creating Your Life from the Inside Out*. New York: Simon & Schuster Source.

Meili, Trisha. 2003. *I Am The Central Park Jogger: A Story of Hope and Possibility*. New York: Scribner.

Metzger, Bruce M. and Roland E. Murphy. 1994. eds. *The New Oxford Annotated Bible*. New York: Oxford University Press.

Osborn, Claudia L. 1998. *Over My Head: A Doctor's Own Story of Head Injury from the Inside Looking Out*. Kansas City: Andrew McMeel Publishing.

Pelzer, Dave. 2000. *Help Yourself: Celebrating the Rewards of Resilience and Gratitude*. New York: Dutton.

Peale, Norman Vincent. 1994. *In God We Trust: A Positive Faith for Troubled Times*. Nashville: Thomas Nelson Publishers.

Pearsall Ph.D., Paul. 2003. *The Beethoven Factor*. Charlottesville: Hampton Roads Publishing.

Pinckaers, Servais. 2001. *Morality: The Catholic View*. South Bend, IN: St. Augustine's Press.

Rahner, Karl. 1983. "Why Does God Allow Us to Suffer?" *Theological Investigations*. 19 (15): 194-208.

Ralston, Aron. 2004. *Between a Rock and a Hard Place*. New York: Atria Books.

Reeve, Christopher. 2002. *Nothing Is Impossible: Reflections on a New Life*. New York: Random House.

Rohn, Jim. The Official Site of Jim Rohn: America's Foremost Business Philosopher. http://www.jimrohn.com.

Rosten, Leo. 1986. *Captain Newman, M.D.* New York: Dell Publishing.

Souhan, Jim. 2001. "Jefferson salutes one of its own with a football game." Minneapolis: *Star Tribune*, September 15.

Shelton, Ron, dir. 1996. *Tin Cup*. DVD. New York: Warner Home Video.

Shyamalan, M. Night, dir. 2002. *Signs*. DVD. Burbank, CA: Touchstone Pictures.

Stevenson, Mary. "Footprints in the Sand", http://www.footprints-inthe-sand.com/index.htm

Stoler, Diane R. and Barbara A. Hill. 1998. *Coping with Mild Traumatic Brain Injury.* Garden City Park, NY: Avery Publishing Group.

Strand, Mike. 2003. *Meditations on Brain Injury.* Minneapolis, MN: Zottola Publishing.

Stone, Oliver, dir. 1999. *Any Given Sunday.* DVD. New York: Warner Home Video.

Tarantino, Quentin, dir. 1994. *Pulp Fiction.* DVD. Burbank, CA: Walt Disney Video.

The American Heritage Dictionary, Second College Edition. 1982. Boston: Houghton Mifflin Co.

The Merriam-Webster's Dictionary. 1997. Springfield, Ma: Merriam-Webster Inc.

Thomson, C.R., trans. 1946. *New Testament and Psalms: The New Testament of Our Lord and Savior Jesus Christ.* Glasgow, Scotland: WM. Collins Sons & Company.

Warren, Rick. 2002. *The Purpose Driven Life.* Grand Rapids, Mi: Zondervan.

Yakin, Boaz, dir. 2001. *Remember the Titans.* DVD. Burbank, CA: Walt Disney Video.

Acknowledgements

I must offer my gratitude to everyone who has been a part of my life, from those who have been with me from the beginning to those who have found a place in my heart. I thank our Lord in Heaven for offering me the purpose that I've discovered. I thank the people at St. Luke's Hospital in Duluth, Minnesota, for their angelic presence as I started my journey, and the three police officers who saved me from the dirty creek; your heroism speaks for itself, representing an honor that can only be God-given.

I give thanks for the true angels I met at Sister Kenny Rehabilitation Institute of Abbott Northwestern Hospital, especially those I came to think of as part of my family: Kristy, Darrel, Jamie, Clint, and Dr. K., along with everyone else who was part of Station 23 and its staff. My therapists: Anita, Elin and Sue, Jackie, Wendy, Kelly, Angie, Lynette, Debbie, and Susan showed me what it means to serve. I am grateful for Mike Schmitz, who showed me that believing in myself was more than enough. And I thank George Montgomery, whose "expertise" added fuel to the fire in my heart. Without it, I may not have been so driven.

I thank my spiritual advisors. Father Kevin Finnegan, whose heart blended passion with strength, inspired me to seek and define my purpose. I thank Bill McDonough, whose teaching about Christian morality has led me to live for the common good. I thank pastor Mac Hammond for his passion, which helped me discover God's will for my life, and for contributing his words, which have surely strengthened mine.

I thank Rick Warren for his phenomenal description of faith at work in *The Purpose Driven Life* and letting me support my writing with some of his. Thanks to Harold Kushner, whose passionate writing style has taught me about life and the essence behind the Twenty-Third Psalm. I'm grateful for the thoughts and insights into life left by Norman Vincent Peale; they are nothing short of miraculous. I am grateful for the usage of Evan Howard's prayers from *Suffering Loss, Seeking Healing*, published by Twenty-Third Publications. And I thank Martha L. Kelfer for allowing me to include the poem "You Are Who You Are," by her husband, Russell Kelfer.

And I thank all my professors at St. Thomas; your passion for education has truly shaped my life and furthered my ability. I would have never been able to succeed as I have without the confidence and support of my advisor, Kim Schumann, who encouraged me to continue my education without letting my disability get the best of me. Your purpose—helping those who lack voices to succeed—is obvious.

I am thankful to Dr. Kent M. Keith, who has graciously allowed me to use his "Paradoxical Commandments" in supporting my story. And I thank Larry Simoneaux of Washington for allowing me to use his heartfelt letter, "To The Teenagers," which appeared in newspaper columns across the country, providing insight to parents and teens alike. I appreciate Douglas Pagels and Blue Mountain Arts for allowing me to reprint his poem about having a positive attitude. I am fortunate to have been introduced to the writings of Christopher Reeve, Kyle Maynard, Trisha Meili, Dr. Phil McGraw, and Aron Ralston, which have offered me a vision of life that's nothing less than extraordinary. I am deeply touched by Oprah Winfrey, who introduced me to Dave Pelzer and Jacqui Saburido, and by her spirit to inspire and serve the world and everyone she encounters.

I am thankful to Kian Dwyer for her positive outlook on life and for introducing me to my writing mentors Milt Adams, Judith Palmateer, and Kellie Hultgren from the Beaver's Pond Press publishing team in Edina, Minnesota. I thank Tom Heller and Jay Monroe for their expertise in designing 23. I offer my gratitude to John Bartos, not only for helping me with the design of my cover, but for his friendship and the confidence he has in me.

I thank Sandy Bernasek from New Jersey, who was my Landmark Forum leader, presented through Landmark Education in 2005. She helped me recognize the reality of what truly was available in my life and I thank Jim Woosley for encouraging me to take part in the three-day event.

And finally, I thank Jennifer Manion who has been a true angel in helping me perfect my words and strengthen my story. Her ability is remarkable and her effort has truly been a price-less gift from the heart. And as I have realized time and time again, most of these people would not have found a place in my life had I not undergone such a trial, and I can't imagine my life without them. The reason behind my experience is apparent and I thank everyone, from the bottom of my heart, for being a part of my life.

About the Author

Nicholas P. Dennen has overcome the challenges of living with a traumatic brain injury, beating tremendous odds despite numerous opinions that had ruled out his ever living a productive life. With perseverance and dedication, Dennen earned a Bachelor of Arts degree in communication studies in 2003 from the University of St. Thomas in St. Paul, MN. He maintains a passion for serving others after experiencing a life-threatening fall in 1998 that left him near death. He has gained inspiration from the many people who gave of themselves wholeheartedly while he underwent a rigorous rehabilitation and relearned the skills necessary for living, such as walking, talking, writing, and just living a productive life. Dennen's attitude has been his greatest asset and he currently works at Methodist Hospital in St. Louis Park, MN, serving patient needs and experiencing the value of life. Dennen gives a percentage of the proceeds from the sale of this book to the Sister Kenny Institute of Abbott Northwestern Hospital and the Brain Injury Association of Minnesota.